PERCY
THROWER'S
guide to

*Colour in
your garden*

Percy Thrower's
GUIDE TO
Colour in your garden

BOOK CLUB ASSOCIATES
London

Contents

First published in 1966 by W. H. & L. Collingridge Ltd.
Second, fully revised edition published in 1976 by
Book Club Associates by arrangement with
The Hamlyn Publishing Group Ltd.,
London · New York · Sydney · Toronto
Astronaut House, Feltham, Middlesex, England

Printed and bound in The Canary Islands by
Litografía A. Romero, S.A.
Santa Cruz de Tenerife, Canary Islands (Spain)
Filmset in England by Tradespools Ltd., Frome, Somerset
in 10 on 11 pt. Monophoto Sabon
D. L. TF. 608 - 1976

ISBN 0 600 33951 3

Colour in Perspective

Much has been said about the design of gardens, and many plans have been published for the guidance of those who wish to make or remodel gardens. In all this advice astonishingly little attention has been paid to the correct use of colour in the garden, yet colour is the most important attribute of many popular flowers.

Our sense of colour is a very personal matter. In some people it is highly developed, others scarcely have it at all. We say of these that they are colour blind, or at any rate blind to some colours, and this is a much more common defect than many people imagine. Partial colour blindness probably accounts for some of the more violent disagreements that occur regarding the correct use, and in particular the correct association, of colours but I am sure they depend also upon much more subtle differences in our individual make up.

For all these reasons it would be foolish for me to be too dogmatic about the use of colour in the garden, for what I like others may dislike. Yet I find that people constantly seek for guidance on this matter just as they seek for guidance in the use of colour in the home, and I think that many of the same principles apply in both garden and home. One can learn a lot by studying what the best home decorators recommend; the colours they are prepared to put together and those they are at pains to keep apart. One can learn, too, from their use of various textures, for texture also enters into the pattern of the garden.

The Colour Wheel

Colours can be considered quite scientifically and objectively in relation to the spectrum. At one extreme are the various shades of red, at the other those of blue and violet, with orange, yellow and green linking them together. There is a device known as a colour wheel (see p. 11) in which the major colours are represented in a circle. The usefulness of this wheel is that it shows, at a glance, which colours can be associated and what the broad effect will be. Colours on opposite sides of the wheel will give strong contrasts. Neighbouring colours on the wheel will give blending effects.

Of course, the colour wheel is quite a crude and simple device. It really only allows for the simplest colours, and makes no provision for the multitude of shades and tints which one finds in plants and upon the clever use of which some of the most delightful colour effects depend. But at least it provides some basic facts for those who do not feel very inventive regarding the handling of colour.

What Does Colour Do?

I think it is just as well to get quite clear in one's mind what purposes colour serves in the garden. As I see it these can all be classified under two headings, and they really have little or nothing to do with one another. Colour may be used to form patterns and it may be used to create moods.

Of course, pattern making in gardens depends upon many other things than colour. Primarily I think it should depend on form; on the shape of beds and borders, the lines created by paths and walls, and the silhouettes of plants, particularly of the more permanent plants such as trees and shrubs.

When the pattern making in a garden depends too heavily upon colour and too little on these dimensional characteristics the weakness is revealed in any monochrome photograph. The garden, which to the eye or in a colour photograph was full of interest, disintegrates and becomes a shapeless mess. We have all seen a good many gardens like that.

Another weakness in the garden that relies too much on colour for its pattern making is that it tends to hold its pattern for too short a period each year. For one of the major difficulties with plant colour, and, incidentally, a major difference between colour in the garden and

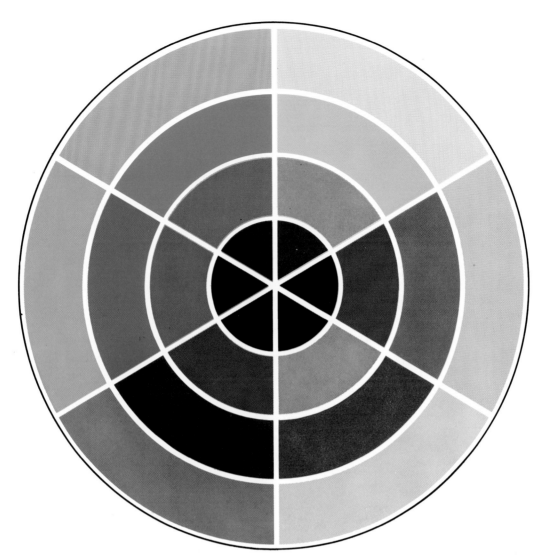

The colour wheel is a diagram designed to show the
relationship of one colour to another. The outer band, band 3
and the inner band all represent gradations of the colours
shown in band 2. Contrasting colours are opposite to each
other, complementary ones are adjacent

colour in the home, is that it does not last. Flowers fade,
some of them all too quickly, and even foliage changes its
hue with the season. So while the home maker can plan
in paints and fabrics which are going to look much the
same from January to December, the garden maker
must work with materials that are changing all the time.
It is all very exciting but it can be a bit puzzling and even,
at times, exasperating.

So much, then, for pattern making with colours. Now
what about the creation of moods? Here we enter the
realm of subjectivity with a vengeance, for what creates
delight in one person quite often creates fury in another.
Yet even here I think some general principles can be
laid down.

Cold Colours and Hot Colours

Blue, for example, is a cool colour (some would even go
so far as to say that it is positively cold). When we are a

little depressed we say that we 'have a fit of the blues'
and though I certainly do not regard blue in the garden
as depressing it has a quietening effect.

By contrast, red and orange are hot colours. They
tend to excite rather than to quiet the mind, and they
excite some people so much that they simply cannot
stand them.

Many pinks are restful but this is not true of all shades
of pink, certainly not of those that contain a fair amount
of blue and which I refer to in more general terms as
puce or magenta. These can be extremely harsh to the
eye, and unless carefully placed in the garden they can
result in frightful colour clashes offensive to most eyes.

Yellows are of so many different qualities that it is
difficult to generalize about them, but the stronger yellows certainly tend to liven up the garden picture. But
again one has to handle them with care for in bad
company they can produce some harsh effects.

Some people say they do not like white flowers but I

11

think they are quite indispensable in the garden. A few well-placed whites in a border will liven up all the other colours without creating any offensive clashes of their own. Together with silver, white is one of the most useful ingredients in the garden maker's palette for breaking the dominance of the strong colours without losing any of their overall brilliance.

The Importance of Green

Green is a different matter altogether. It is the most useful of all the garden colours because it will harmonize with them all and tone down the harshness of the most aggressive. But, unlike white, it does lower the general level of brilliance. Again a monochrome photograph can be very revealing of what I am trying to express. Take such a picture of a garden in which there are a lot of white flowers and the result will certainly be lively whatever else it may be. Take another photograph of a garden in which green predominates and the result may be soft and hazy to the point of dullness.

But never underestimate the importance of green. If you look at floral decorations today you cannot fail to note the popularity of combinations of green and yellow, pale yellows in particular, and lime green. Do not forget that there are all sorts of green just as there are all sorts of red, blue, yellow and all the other colours. If you want something really charming and restful and a little different, you might even consider planning some part of the garden entirely in shades of green.

Where Colours can be Used Freely

There are some gardens, and some places in the garden, where colour can be used more freely than in others. Bedding-out schemes are usually conceived in terms of massed colour and often for quite contrary reasons. In very small gardens or in formal town gardens cheerful bedding-out plants provide the best way of giving gaiety to what might otherwise be a rather dull picture, and as they must be changed with the seasons, the picture itself is a changing one. In a big garden one could contrive such changes by placing plants of different seasons near to one another so that, as the flowers of one fade, the flowers of another open, but that is not possible unless there is plenty of space.

Bedding-out plants are also very appropriate in public parks because there the aim is to make the maximum effect. It is like an orchestra playing crescendo; it is all very exciting and fine so long as one has not got to stay with it too long – and public parks are places to visit rather than to live in. Incidentally, the cost, in terms of plants and labour and resources, such as frames and greenhouses, for maintaining that crescendo of colour, would be quite beyond most amateur gardeners.

Colour can be laid on heavily in the herbaceous

Shrubs, herbaceous plants and annuals are all cleverly used in this mixed planting where colour and texture are important. Dwarf conifers make a perfect foil for the hydrangea and lead the eye to other features

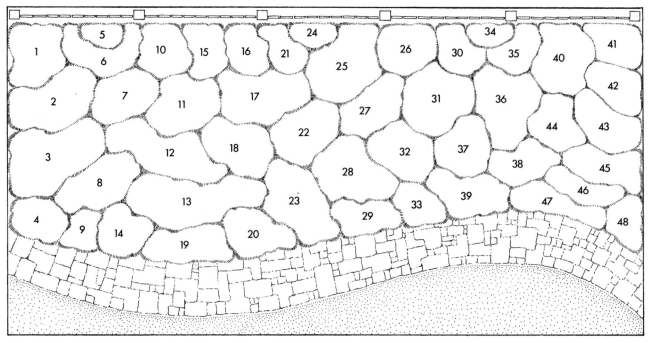

Plants in this 8-ft (2·5-m) wide mixed border, designed for an all-summer display, are: 1. *Hibiscus coelestris*. 2. *Helenium* Wyndley. 3. *Astilbe* Federsee. 4. *Gaillardia* Mandarin. 5. *Rosa* Zephirine Drouhin. 6. *Aster* Winston Churchill. 7. *Chrysanthemum maximum* Esther Read. 8. *Aster amellus* King George. 9. *Lavandula spica*. 10. *Acanthus mollis latifolius*. 11. *Caryopteris clandonensis* Kew Blue. 12. *Anemone hybrida* Louise Uhink. 13. *Agapanthus* Headbourne Hybrids. 14. *Geranium sanguineum lancastriense splendens*. 15. *Fuchsia magellanica riccartonii*. 16. *Delphinium* Ann Page. 17. *Hemerocallis* Golden Chimes. 18. *Lilium candidum*. 19. *Bergenia cordifolia* Ballawley. 20. *Monarda didyma* Cambridge Scarlet. 21. *Phlox* Eventide. 22. *Rosa* Nevada. 23. *Polygonum bistorta superbum*. 24. *Clematis* Comtesse de Bouchaud. 25. *Cimicifuga racemosa*. 26. *Kniphofia* Royal

border, too, and this was the traditional way of doing things, with the plants in bold groups of a kind. This kind of planting is still carried out in some large gardens and public parks, but it is not, in my opinion, the best way to handle herbaceous plants in ordinary gardens, mainly because there is not the space to get these bold effects. Even if one does, by hook or by crook, contrive them they tend to be short lived. Not many herbaceous perennials flower for more than four or five weeks at a time, and so considerable ingenuity in grouping is necessary if the display of the herbaceous border is to be continuous for several months. Of course, this can be overcome to some extent by mixing temporary plants – bedding plants and annuals and dahlias – with the herbaceous plants, but there is a limit to what can be achieved in an average private garden.

In such places I think it is better to plant herbaceous perennials in ones and twos, or at most in groups of three, and not to worry at all if there are considerable stretches of green where plants have already flowered or are yet to come into flower. Such a border cannot compare with more colourful ones for sheet excitement, but it is much more restful and, if I may use the phrase, 'liveable with'.

Tree and Shrub Colour

All this is even more true of tree and shrub colour. Some of the very large gardens contrive quite fantastic colour displays with rhododendrons and azaleas, but usually such gardens tend to be colourful for a brief period only.

They have their heyday in May and are pretty dull for the rest of the year, though some contrive a second burst of colour with hydrangeas in summer.

This brings to my mind a rather unusual rhododendron garden planned by an amateur who is very sensitive to colour. It is conceived entirely in shades of blue and yellow with occasional white to liven things up. Nothing else obtrudes at this particular season though other colour effects, not dependent upon rhododendrons, appear at other times of the year. This kind of planning requires great forethought and considerable knowledge of the precise colours and flowering times, and the heights and rates of growth of plants, but it can be immense fun and is well worth doing if one has the time and the inclination.

Rhododendron and azalea colour can be rather hot and tiring, as any reader who visits a garden where these splendid shrubs are planted widely and in a conventional way will see for himself. One must be especially careful about colour groupings, too, for a colour like bluey-pink – which is found in azaleas – can be an intrusion when seen against a background of, say, coppery-orange.

How to Make a Plan

There are many ways of approaching the problem of preparing colour schemes for one's own garden. Some people do a lot of preliminary paper work and some do not. I am in the latter category but then I have had a good many years at the game. It is not difficult for me to

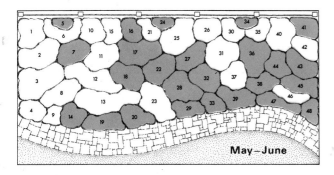

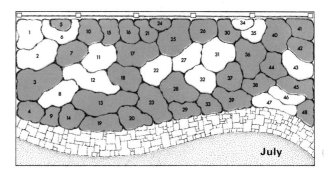

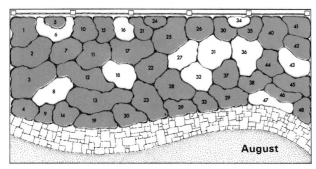

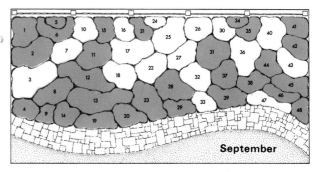

Standard. 27. *Papaver* Marcus Perry. 28. *Hosta sieboldiana*. 29. *Ajuga reptans* Burgundy Glow. 30. *Achillea filipendulina* Gold Plate. 31. *Aster* Apple Blossom. 32. *Geranium psilostemon*. 33. *Eryngium bourgatii*. 34. *Lonicera periclymenum belgica*. 35. *Galtonia candicans*. 36. *Senecio laxifolius*. 37. *Physostegia virginiana* Vivid. 38. *Sidalcea* Croftway Red. 39. *Nepeta faassenii*. 40. *Heliopsis* Golden Plume. 41. *Potentilla fruticosa*

Katherine Dykes. 42. Montbretia Star of the East. 43. *Trollius* Goldquelle. 44. *Santolina incana*. 45. *Hosta fortunei albo-picta*. 46. *Sedum spectabile*. 47. *Dianthus* Mrs Sinkins. 48. *Heuchera* Bressingham Hybrids

The four charts (above) refer to the plan on the opposite page. The coloured areas indicate when the plants will be in flower

visualize the colours, heights and shapes of the various plants and to bear in mind their respective seasons of beauty. I build up schemes in my mind's eye and then I go out and turn them into reality in the garden. I do not carry out a great deal of formal planning on paper, though for future reference I make notes of schemes I have liked in my own garden, or in gardens I have visited or seen in pictures.

I fancy most amateur gardeners, and particularly beginners, will find it easier to do a bit more paper work before they actually set to work in the garden. One simple and effective way of doing this is to draw a fairly large outline plan to scale of the borders or beds you wish to plant and then, on separate slips of paper or cardboard, write down the names of the plants you fancy. There should be one strip (in practice it may be better to make it an oval or a circle) for each plant or group of plants of the same variety. In addition to the name, write down on this slip of paper the height of the plant, its flowering season and its colour or, better still, if you want to be really thorough, put a splash of the colour on the slip with a paintbrush.

Then you can arrange your slips on your outline plan, rather like putting a jigsaw puzzle together. You can see just how the colours are going to come together. It will be possible to check that colours meant to coincide in time really will do so, for many an otherwise excellent scheme has gone awry simply through neglect of this elementary matter. You will also be able to make sure that a tall plant will not hide the display of a short one,

but if possible will provide an effective background to it. Of course, it does not so much matter in a herbaceous border if an earlier flowering 'shorty' is later screened by a later flowering plant of greater height; indeed sometimes this can be the most effective means of masking what might otherwise by ugly and untidy blanks in the borders.

Viewpoints from the House

All planning schemes should be considered from the viewpoint from which they will be seen most frequently. In small gardens this is more often than not the house and it will pay to make frequent visits to this and survey the garden from the principal windows, trying to visualize just what the schemes you are planning will look like from these. Do not forget the kitchen window, for it may well be the room in which your wife spends a good part of each day and she deserves as pleasant an outlook as possible.

The Dingle in Quarry Park, Shrewsbury, which was in my charge for many years, is an example of a garden particularly difficult to colour plan, because it can be looked at from all sides and in many places from above too. You get things right from one viewpoint only to discover that they are hopelessly wrong from another. This is the kind of problem that only gets solved by experience, by trying one arrangement and then another until eventually everything falls into place according to your liking.

15

Woodland, Streamside and Rock Gardens

I think colour needs to be used fairly sparingly in the woodland garden and by pool and streamside. These should all be cool and restful places not overburdened with hot and tiring colour. A woodland path with azaleas lining it on one side can be a really lovely scene, a study in pink and mauve with plenty of green to set it off. Put a strong yellow into that and you would kill it completely.

Streamside gardens should always be planted with an eye to form as well as colour. For example, to provide interest in the middle distance such plants as the giant cow parsnip or heracleum can be used, provided the scale of this planting is appropriate to their size. This has flat heads of white flowers and good leaves as well as a rather statuesque form, and it fits in well with low-growing primulas and other small plants along the side of a stream. Strong colour contrasts which would destroy the peace of the picture should be avoided.

Rock gardens need quite a lot of thought. They can so easily be a bit gaudy and brash in spring and then rather dull for the rest of the year. Generally the colours want to be well mixed and spread over as long a season as possible. Too much purple aubrieta and yellow alyssum can upset the balance, though I am a great admirer of both flowers and like to see the deep yellow and pale alyssums planted together for colour harmony.

Planting Walls

Then there is the problem of planting walls. Stone walls and weathered timber seldom present much difficulty for if they are in some shade of grey, as they usually are, that is a neutral colour which will go with anything. But brick can be difficult and the redder it is the greater the difficulty so far as colour planning is concerned. For example, the orange-scarlet-berried *Pyracantha coccinea lalandei* can clash horribly with some brick walls and the only saving grace with that splendid wall shrub in such a situation is that it grows quickly and soon covers the brickwork with its evergreen leaves.

Honeysuckles go with red brick and so does the winter jasmine. One has to be careful with roses, particularly pink and red roses, but the yellows, buffs and whites should be all right.

The Special Problem of Red

I have already referred to the special problem of red in any part of the garden. Someone has said that reds burn holes in the landscape and I know exactly what they mean. So many reds simply do not blend in well and the eye treats them as something extraneous to the rest. The hybrid tea rose Super Star is a case in point. It can be surrounded by green plants or associated with white

A large clump of orange-flowered montbretia is planted here with russet heleniums to provide a fiery display. The colour is picked up further along the border by more heleniums and an edging of French marigolds

or some of the softer yellows and buffs, but it is not easy to get it really into the picture.

In summer bedding scarlet salvia is much more difficult than red geranium simply because it produces so much bloom that practically none of its own foliage remains to be seen. Even the best of the red geraniums retain plenty of visible green leaves throughout the height of their flowering season. I always use plenty of silver foliage along with the red in all my summer colour schemes. *Centaurea gymnocarpa* and *Cineraria maritima* (or, to give it its most up-to-date name, *Senecio cineraria*) are invaluable silvers, and I also bring in soft golden-yellow in the plant known as golden feather which, is, in fact, *Chrysanthemum parthenium aureum*, sometimes catalogued as *Matricaria eximia aurea*.

Bark and Foliage Effects

In winter one an take all the colour one can get and there is never really enough of it. Many of the bark effects can be very lovely, the yellows of some of the willows, the reds of the dogwood and the grey or blue-whites of the whitewash brambles (*Rubus cockburnianus*). These are all colours which light up beautifully in the winter sun.

In winter, too, evergreen shrubs come into their own. For this reason evergreens should be placed very carefully in mixed plantations and shrub borders. Remember that you are planning here for two totally different pictures. In summer, when all the shrubs are in leaf, all will merge in together but in winter, when the deciduous shrubs are bare skeletons, the evergreens will stand out alone. They must be placed so that they look right then and make an entirely new grouping of their own.

Foliage plants of all kinds, herbaceous as well as shrubby, can be tremendously important in giving firmness and permanence to the scenes one is attempting to create. Some herbaceous plants have an almost architectural or sculptured appearance, the hostas, rodgersias, and acanthus more so than any others, I think. Their leaves are large and well formed, and the colours are pleasing and harmonize with almost anything else. There is plenty of colour variation in hostas, too, grey, blue and green, as well as silver and gold variegated varieties which can be very effective indeed.

Colour in Spring

One thing you have to remember when composing any early spring picture for the garden is that, apart from a few evergreens, there will be no green from the trees. They will be bare and so any green you need must come from the grass or from the foliage of the plants themselves. That is one reason why I prefer some of the wild tulips and the hybrids from wild tulips such as the Water Lily tulips (*Tulipa kaufmanniana* and its varieties) and Peacock tulips (*T. greigii* and its varieties) to the Darwin and Cottage tulips because many of them have quite decorative and interesting leaves, often striped with maroon or chocolate.

Many people like what are called garden tulips but I

An effective waterside planting using the large leaves and creamy flowers of *Rodgersia aesculifolia* as a backing for the candelabra-like flowers of *Primula* Inverewe

find them rather difficult to place. They are too stiff and set for my liking, especially when planted in blocks of colour as they usually are. Personally, I plant them individually or in small groups here and there for a touch of colour.

Just as I find a personal difficulty with the conventional massed tulips, so do I have difficulty in reconciling myself to wallflowers massed to colour. Broadly we have seven basic colours to work with, the blood red, fiery red, orange, deep yellow, pale yellow, purple and the Eastern Queen type of rose. I have never been able to separate these to my liking, and so I generally plant orange, yellow and blood red all mixed together and this seems to me to be an eye catcher.

Another point in spring bedding where I find myself at variance with general practice is in the use of edgings. For summer there is plenty of choice of good edging plants. A compact lobelia or alyssum or *Centaurea candidissima* can be used, or the golden feather (*Chrysanthemum parthenium aureum*), to which I have already referred, and any of these can easily be kept neat and tidy. But for spring there is no such choice. Forget-me-

Flowers and foliage in white, cream and green are invaluable. Plumes of *Aruncus sylvester* are a backing for phlox with *Miscanthus sinensis variegatus* in the front

not is too loose unless you are fortunate enough to get a really good strain. Polyanthus makes a poor edging though it is magnificent occupying a bed on its own. Arabis cannot be relied upon, so I always take the polyanthus or the wallflowers right out to the edge of the bed.

Colour Combinations

One spring combination that always looks lovely is grape hyacinth planted under pink almond or cherry. Actually, with me, the almond flowers a bit too early for the grape hyacinth and a Japanese cherry such as Kanzan or Shirofugen is just right, but in other places the almond and grape hyacinth combination might be the one to go for.

In May and early June we get the lovely and, in many instances, quite unique colours of the bearded irises. They all blend together admirably, but you need enough of the brighter blues and the whites and yellows to liven up some of the more sombre purple, mulberry and smoky-violet shades. Irises will go along with other flowers in the herbaceous borders, but the most beautiful effects I have seen with them have always been in iris gardens, or even quite small iris beds which they occupy more or less in isolation.

Water as a Mirror

So far I have said nothing about water in the garden except in so far as it was implied in my comments about the streamside garden. But that was running water. Still water is quite another thing for, provided it is reasonably clear, it introduces an entirely new element to the garden – reflection. Water is to the garden as a mirror is to a room. It increases its apparent size and at the same time captivates the eye with new angles on familiar scenes. Water in the garden even captures the sky and brings it down to earth, for on a clear day the pool will be blue and on a dull day it will be grey. If there are billowing white clouds up above, you will have the whiteness added to the picture you have composed in your garden.

This is what nature gives you immediately you introduce still, clear water to your garden. Art and artifice can give you more. Plants and ornaments and even garden furniture can be placed so that their images, too, are captured in the still surface of the pool.

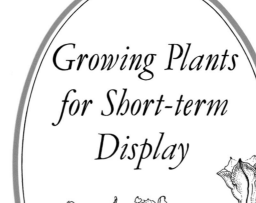

Growing Plants for Short-term Display

It could be said that all ornamental plants are grown in gardens for display, for they are certainly there to be looked at, and most gardeners will want to place them and grow them so that they look their best. Here I am concerned with a rather special aspect of gardening for display – the cultivation of plants that are intended to maintain colour for a while, and then be removed to make way for other plants that will keep up the display as continuously and effectively as possible. This kind of gardening is immensely important in public parks and is quite practicable in small gardens, too, because the numbers of plants required will not be great and many of them can be raised at home.

The plants required for display gardening can be broadly divided into those that are raised annually from seed (they are not all annuals), and those that are raised from cuttings or divisions. The seed plants can themselves be subdivided into those that need to be raised under glass and those that can be sown out of doors, but there is no sharp dividing line between the two as much depends on locality and time of sowing.

Half-hardy Perennials from Seed

I will take these first because most of them need to be sown first. Under this heading come the tuberous-rooted begonias, which are now so popular, heliotrope, many verbenas (though I raise two of my special favourites, Lawrence Johnston and Loveliness, from cuttings), dwarf bedding dahlias, and lobelia, the scarlet salvia (now available in other colours), the fibrous-rooted begonias and antirrhinums – though most gardeners think of them and treat them as annuals. All these plants need to be sown in March; in fact if a temperature of 16° to 18°C (60° to 65°F) can be maintained with fair certainty, it is worth sowing the antirrhinums, begonias and salvias in the latter half of February, as bigger plants will be obtained by this means. But it is necessary to think ahead and remember that it will be unsafe to plant

outdoors until late May except in some very mild seaside places, and that plants from February sowings, if they have grown well, will almost certainly need to be grown individually in small pots for the last few weeks before they go out. At this stage 40 or 50 plants can take up quite a lot of room so it is no use sowing very early if this space, under protection of some kind, is not going to be available

In theory all these half-hardy perennials could be kept from year to year; in practice it is seldom worth while to perpetuate any of them except the tuberous-rooted begonias, which can be stored dry during the winter in a frostproof cupboard, and so will present no problems at a time when greenhouse space will almost certainly be needed for other things. The rest can be raised so easily and cheaply each year from seed that this is the simplest course to adopt.

Half-hardy Annuals

Under this heading are included a great many of the most popular summer bedding plants: ageratum, asters, arctotis, Giant Chabaud carnations, cleome, cosmos, *Dianthus heddewigii*, matricaria, French and African marigolds, *Mesembryanthemum criniflorum*, nemesia, nicotiana, petunia, portulaca, *Phlox drummondii*, annual rudbeckia, stocks, *Tagetes signata*, ursinia, venidium and zinnia. It is an impressive list and of some kinds, notably the asters, marigolds, petunias and zinnias, there are innumerable varieties so that there really is something for every place and every need.

Raising Half-hardy Plants from Seed

The germination and subsequent treatment of all these half-hardy plants to be grown from seed is very similar and there is no need to distinguish between the annuals and the perennials. All will germinate rapidly in a temperature of 16° to 18°C (60° to 65°F) and some of the hardier kinds, such as the asters, stocks, zinnias and annual scabious, will be satisfied with 13°C (55°F). These can, in fact, be sown outdoors in late April or early May when the average temperature should be in that region.

It helps a lot if a propagating frame, however small, or even a box covered with glass, is available in the greenhouse, for in this it will be much easier to maintain a steady temperature without much expense. If electricity is laid on an electric air-warming cable can be placed in the frame or box, or you can buy a small propagator complete with electric heater. This does not necessarily mean that no heating will be required in the house itself, but the heating can almost certainly be at a lower level, and the difference in cost between maintaining a greenhouse at 7°C (45°F) and maintaining it at 16°C (60°F) is quite astonishing.

Late February and early March is the time for most of the seed sowing, but the stocks and asters can wait until late March and the zinnias until early April.

Either John Innes seed compost or one of the soilless composts based on peat can be used, both for seed germination and for growing on, but the soilless compost needs less watering than John Innes compost. The compost can be placed in ordinary wooden seed boxes, in plastic seed trays or in pots or pans, which may be either clay or plastic, but in all cases should be provided with ample drainage holes or slits. Waterlogged compost will kill seedlings as quickly as anything.

Level off the compost with a straight-edge and then press it lightly with a piece of smooth flat wood to get a firm, level surface. Scatter the seed thinly over this and then sift a little of the compost over the seed (but very small seeds, such as those of the begonia, need no covering). Finally, place a sheet of glass and one of paper over each box or pan.

Germination may take from a week to three weeks according to variety and temperature available. The paper coverings should be removed as soon as the seedlings are seen, and the glass a day or so later. A week or ten days later the seedlings will probably be ready for pricking out, i.e. they must be very carefully transplanted so that each seedling is properly spaced and has room to grow into a sturdy little plant. The same kind of compost as that used for germination will be suitable, and as a rule it is most convenient to prick out into seed boxes, spacing the seedlings about $1\frac{1}{2}$ in (4 cm) apart each way. At this spacing an ordinary wooden seed box measuring 14 by $8\frac{1}{2}$ in (35 × 21 cm) will hold 54 seedlings. If you are dealing with much smaller numbers you can prick out into pots or pans, but they do not pack quite so well on the greenhouse staging or in the frame.

Pricking Out

It is worth taking a good deal of trouble to prick out the seedlings with as little injury to their roots as possible. If the work is done really early this will not be difficult, and they can be lifted a few at a time from the seed boxes or pans with a wooden tally and then, after being care-

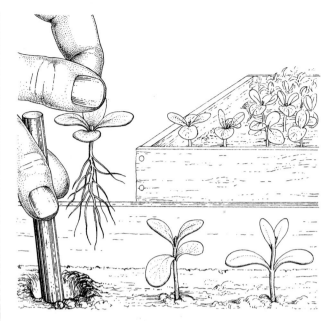

Pricking out, the method of transplanting seedlings when they have germinated. It is important to do this carefully, handling the seedlings only by their leaves

fully singled out, can be planted in holes made with a pointed stick known as a dibber. But if for some reason the seedlings have grown so much that they cannot be lifted easily in this way, it is better to tip out the whole contents of the seed box or pot and then carefully disentangle the roots, than to risk breaking a lot of them.

Make the soil firm around the roots with the fingers or a dibber and, when a box or pan has been filled with seedlings, water it thoroughly using a watering can fitted with a fine rose. This will keep the seedlings fresh while they are getting established, and will settle the soil closely around their roots.

The pricked-out seedlings should then be placed on the greenhouse staging. It may be necessary to shade them for a few days, especially if the weather is bright; certainly they should not be allowed to flag badly at this stage. They must be watered before the soil becomes dry, but too much water at first may check rather than assist growth.

Planting Out

The planting out of these half-hardy plants can seldom be done with safety before late May because of the danger of sharp night frosts before that date. In cool areas it may even be necessary to delay until the first or second week in June. Only in very mild places, particularly maritime ones, can early or mid-May planting be contemplated.

In any case the seedlings should not go direct from warm greenhouse to cold outdoors. They must have a fortnight or so of acclimatization or hardening off. This is most conveniently given in a frame, because the protecting light can be left on if frost threatens or be removed altogether if the weather is mild.

A great many half-hardy plants are kept in the boxes

Polyanthuses interplanted with forget-me-nots, pansies, double daisies and tulips form a mass of colour

in which they were pricked out right up to the time of planting out. This is all right as long as they do not get starved or overcrowded, but if they show any signs of either they should be potted individually. Quite small pots will do, 2½ or 3 in (6.5 or 8 cm) in diameter, but this time a rather richer compost must be used, either the John Innes potting compost or one of the soilless composts.

Sowing Out of Doors

The outdoor sowings may include three groups of plants. First there are hardy annuals. They can be sown where they are to flower and later the seedlings can be thinned out so that they are not overcrowded. Usually the seedlings transplant quite well, so the thinnings, if lifted carefully with plenty of roots, can be used to fill in gaps. March and April are good months for sowing hardy annuals, but even May is not too late, and from such sowings plants will be obtained that will flower in August and September.

It is also possible to sow some of the hardiest of hardy annuals, plants such as larkspur, calendula, eschscholzia, nigella, clarkia, godetia and candytuft, in late or early September. The seedlings will be sturdy enough to overwinter without protection and they will be ready to flower the following summer well ahead of the spring-sown annuals. But there is risk of considerable loss of seedlings if the soil is badly drained or the winter is a very cold one.

In addition to the genuine hardy annuals, there are some half-hardy annuals that can be sown outdoors in late April or May, notably asters and zinnias as described on p. 28. The plants will flower later than those raised under glass but that can be very useful. One does not want all the colour from annuals to come in June, July and early August with nothing to follow.

Plants for Winter, Spring and Early Summer

All these annuals and half-hardy bedding plants are summer flowering. For winter and spring it is necessary to turn to two other groups, the hardy biennials and early-flowering perennials that grow quickly from seed. These include wallflowers (*Cheiranthus cheiri*), the Siberian wallflower *(C. allionii)*, polyanthus, double daises, pansies, forget-me-nots and Canterbury bells.

All can be raised from seed, the seedlings being planted out in rows in a bed reserved for this purpose, and grown on until the summer-flowering plants have been cleared away when these, the spring-bedding plants, can be put in their place. But there generalizations must cease and each plant must receive its own appropriate treatment.

Polyanthus needs to be sown earliest, if possible in February or March, in a greenhouse or frame with a temperature of around 13°C (55°F). Subsequently, the resulting seedlings are pricked out into boxes and later planted out, much as if they were half-hardy annuals, except that they are planted in a nursery bed, not in a display bed. They may begin to produce a few flower buds in the autumn, but these should be picked off so that the plants build up good crowns to flower really freely the following spring.

Next in order of sowing time come the wallflower and Siberian wallflower, double daisies (bellis) and Canterbury bells, all to be sown in May and June.

Forget-me-nots grow so rapidly that there is no need to sow them before the latter half of June. Pansies I sow in late June or July. There is a specially useful type of pansy known as winter-flowering, which starts to flower very early. I use it a lot in my spring displays.

All these plants get the same subsequent treatment and go into their flowering beds in the autumn as soon as these have been cleared of summer occupants; but with wallflowers it does pay to get all planting finished in September, as then the plants are far less likely to suffer in winter.

Display Plants from Cuttings

Some of the finest summer-flowering display plants are perennials which can be conveniently and cheaply raised from cuttings. Into this category come geraniums (pelargoniums, to be correct), marguerites, the grey-leaved *Centaurea gymnocarpa* and *Cineraria maritima*, penstemons, bedding calceolarias, fuchsias, chrysan-

Of the spring flowers, few can surpass the polyanthuses for sheer brilliance of colour – from pure white to pale and deep yellow, orange, crimson, magenta, pale and deep blue, and most have contrasting centres

themums and dahlias. I say more about the last two later in the book, and I shall confine myself to the others here.

Cuttings are most conveniently taken in August and September, for then the plants will be growing freely in the summer beds and a few shoots can be cut from each without being missed. Firm, non-flowering shoots are best, but if there are not enough of these any young growths can be used after removal of the flowers.

The cuttings should be 3 or 4 in (8 or 10 cm) long. Each is cut straight through at the bottom, just below a joint, i.e. where a leaf or leaves are attached to the stem. The bottom leaves are removed, the base of the cutting is dipped in hormone rooting powder, which can be bought from any dealer in garden sundries, and then the cuttings are inserted in holes about 1 in (2·5 cm) deep made with a dibber in sandy soil. A good compost for cuttings consists of equal parts (by volume) of soil, coarse sand and peat, but quite a lot will root in ordinary garden soil with a little sand and peat raked in. Every August I root some geranium cuttings out of doors without any protection at all, but by September it is better to put the cuttings in pots or boxes so that they can be brought into a frostproof greenhouse or frame directly frost threatens.

Penstemons and calceolarias are nearly hardy and can be overwintered in a frame without any artificial heat. Violas can be grown in the same way, but nowadays there are such excellent seed strains available that not many gardeners bother with cuttings.

Geranium and fuchsia cuttings root very quickly and indicate when they have done so by starting to grow again. This is the signal to tap them out of their pots (or lift them if they were rooted outdoors) and pot them individually. Quite small pots will do, 2½ in (6·5 cm) for fuchsias, 3 in (8 cm) or 3½ in (9 cm) for the geraniums. Either John Innes potting compost or one of the soilless composts will do for all of them, and the best place for them is on the staging in a light greenhouse with a minimum temperature of 7°C (45°F).

Cuttings also root readily in March and April so if you are short of plants you can insert some more then. This is what I always do with two of my favourite carpeting plants, the verbenas Loveliness and Lawrence Johnston. I root some cuttings in August and September, overwinter the resulting plants in the greenhouse, and then take more cuttings from them in early spring.

The only difference in the treatment of spring cuttings is that they need a little warmth (a temperature of 16 to 18°C [60 to 65°F] is ideal) and root more readily in a propagating frame or a box covered with a pane of glass – anything, in fact, that will reduce air circulation and keep the air around them moist.

Forms of Training

I have already said a good deal about the cultivation of bedding plants, but before passing on to describe some of the ways in which they may be used in the garden, I want to mention the training of plants, which can make so much difference to their effectiveness. Amateur gardeners, I think, are too ready to accept plants as they are. The professionals know that some plants, though beautiful in their natural habit, can be made to serve other useful purposes by being trained.

Standards

I am especially fond of fuchsias and, though I've grown a great many as bushes with no more regulation of their natural habit than to make it even bushier by occasionally pinching out the tips of shoots, I've also grown a lot of standard fuchsias.

These are quite easy to form and if you have a greenhouse you can do it for yourself. Start with cuttings in August. When these are rooted and potted, place a cane to each plant and keep the main growth tied to this so that it is absolutely straight and erect.

All side growths are removed until the main stem is about 5 ft (1·5 m) high, and then the top of the plant is pinched out to make it branch. What you want are six or eight good branches near the top and any others in excess of this can be removed. When these side growths are themselves 6 or 8 in (15 or 20 cm) long, they are pinched again to make even more branches, and so produce a really good 'head' of growth at the top of the main stem.

If the fuchsias are kept in a greenhouse with a temperature of around 13°C (55°F) they will go on growing all the winter and so, by the time the summer bedding is to be put out in late May or early June, they will be good, big plants, very useful for dotting here and there among the shorter plants to give height and variety to the beds. But they do need a lot of water during the summer, and to keep them flowering well into the autumn they should be given feeds of liquid manure.

Once formed these standards can be kept for years. They are lifted and potted in the autumn and brought under cover, but no attempt is made to keep them growing, as it was the first year when they were formed. Instead, they are permitted to take a rest until late February, when they are pruned, all side growths being shortened to 2 or 3 in (5 or 8 cm). They are then knocked out of their pots, most of the soil is teased from their roots with a pointed stick, and they are repotted, watered and kept in a cool greenhouse to start them into growth.

Geraniums, as well as heliotrope (cherry pie), can be trained as standards in the same way and can be very decorative.

Pegging Down

There are other plants, naturally low growing, which can be made even more useful by a little training and pegging down. This can be done with annual phlox, verbena and ivy-leaved geraniums. If some fairly stout galvanized wire is cut into 6-in (15-cm) lengths, and these are bent like hairpins, they can be put over the trailing shoots and pushed into the soil to hold them where they are required to cover the soil with a continuous carpet of growth and flowers.

Bedding Plant Associations

Everyone will want to work out original schemes with bedding plants, but I intend now to describe some that I find pleasing for summer display.

I like to make a groundwork of rich purple heliotrope (I use the variety Marine) and edge it with silver- and green-leaved geraniums, for which I use the variety Little Dandy. Then I put in one or two standard plants of a free-flowering deep red fuchsia named Lord Leverhulme, to grow above the heliotrope, and a few plants of *Calocephalus brownii* (syn. *Leucophyta brownii*) which

Half-hardy annuals in variety lend themselves to being planted in many situations but particularly in sunny parts of the garden. In this paved area, mesembryanthemum, petunia, dimorphotheca, alyssum and tagetes are attractively mingled to create a spectacular effect

has thin, silver stems and can be trained to form erect columns of growth.

I find the scarlet salvia the hardest of all colours to place because it is so brilliant and there is so little green with it. So to break up this mass of dazzling colour I use *Fuchsia* Mrs Marshall grown as a standard, some big

25

plants of silver-leaved *Centaurea gymnocarpa*, orange-flowered cannas with green leaves and an edging of white alyssum or Little Dandy geranium.

I also use *Fuchsia* Mrs Marshall, but bushy plants, not standards, with the red fibrous-rooted *Begonia semperflorens* and bring in *Chrysanthemum ptarmicaeflorum* for silver, and golden feather, *Chrysanthemum parthenium aureum* (syn. *Matricaria eximia aurea*) for yellowish-green, with *Iresine aurea* for a stronger yellow foliage colour.

The peach-coloured *Begonia* Helen Harmes is one of my favourites. With this I mix the red and purple *Fuchsia* Brutus, dark red *Iresine lindeni* and silver chrysanthemum, and surround it all with the dark blue *Lobelia* Crystal Palace.

Another splendid begonia is Thousand Wonders, with pale pink flowers. With this I plant the bright red and bronze *Iresine herbstii brillantissima*, silver pyrethrum and *Lobelia* Cambridge Blue, and I put in a few plants of *Fuchsia* Thalia, which has red flowers and bronzy-green leaves.

Some of the red varieties of *Begonia semperflorens* have dark bronze leaves, and a silver-leaved plant such as *Cineraria maritima* (syn. *Senecio cineraria*) or silver chrysanthemum livens these up most attractively. For further foliage colour I may add yellow *Iresine aurea*.

I like to make beds of salmon-pink geraniums with an edging of *Lobelia* Cambridge Blue and a few silver-leaved dot plants. With scarlet geraniums I bring in both silver and golden variegated plants, including the tall *Abutilon striatum thompsonii* which makes a standard above the geraniums. Here again I can use *Fuchsia* Mrs Marshall as a standard, and I edge it all with white alyssum or Little Dandy geranium. With regard to geraniums, these can now be raised cheaply from seed for bedding purposes, F_1 hybrids like the Carefree strain – available as a mixture or in separate colours – and the scarlet Sprinter having proved their worth, while new ones which come into flower earlier are Matador, Candy and Shiva, all with the prefix Del Greco and salmon-cerise, rose and scarlet colouring respectively.

For spring display I rely mainly on polyanthus, wallflowers and winter-flowering pansies.

The wallflowers I grow either in random mixture, all the colours together, or else in quite separate beds of colour. I have never been very happy with two or three varieties mixed in blocks of colour in a bed.

I have tried polyanthus in separate colours, but from seed there is usually some variation and I have come to the conclusion that they look better mixed.

I also like the winter-flowering pansies mixed, especially in large beds or borders, but in smaller beds I do use separate colours of which there is a wide choice such as pale blue, golden-yellow, deep purple, crimson and bronze.

Around the terrace of the author's house is a colourful summer-bedding display. The blue edging of lobelia is backed by orange French marigolds and red geraniums interplanted with *Senecio cineraria*

A Selection of Annuals

For convenience annuals are divided into two categories, hardy and half-hardy, but it must be understood that the division is an arbitrary one. In fact, no hard and fast line can be drawn, for what is hardy in one part of the country might be half-hardy in another. Moreover, though it is broadly true that hardy annuals are sown outdoors where they are to flower, whereas half-hardy annuals are sown under glass to be planted out when danger of frost is past, there are exceptions on both sides. Sweet alyssum is fully hardy, yet millions of plants are raised commercially in greenhouses each spring and sold to the public in boxes. Asters and zinnias are genuine half-hardy annuals, yet both can be sown outdoors in late April and early May in many parts of Britain, and some of the most successful growers invariably treat zinnias in this way, contending that the plants do better grown cool and without any break. Also, this way you avoid trouble with damping off (botrytis) and foot rot, which can cause trouble with this flower under glass, with the rotting of the stems and the decay of the roots.

Nearly all annuals like sun and most have a very wide tolerance of soils, though they do best in those of rather open texture in which good crumbly seed beds can be prepared. They are easy to grow, too, and as they will be in full flower within a very short time, they are ideal plants with which to furnish the new garden while more permanent plans are being prepared. Practically all you need to do to annuals, once they have been planted and thinned out, is to keep them free from the competition of weeds and to pick off the faded flowers before seeds begin to form. Weeds will starve the plants and make the beds untidy. Plants that are allowed to form seeds will soon stop flowering.

The following lists of hardy and half-hardy annuals can all be recommended for their colour. In the main I have not listed varieties as there are so many of these, often varying from seed house to seed house. These will be found in the different catalogues together with details of heights. Some of the plants mentioned are, in fact, perennials but are usually grown as half-hardy annuals in this country.

Hardy Annuals

Alyssum (Sweet Alyssum). Most gardeners know this as *A. maritimum* although it is now correctly *Lobularia maritima*. It is one of the most popular of all edging plants and also one of the easiest to grow, providing colour from spring to autumn. On a light soil, once you have sown alyssum, you will probably never need to sow it again as self-sown seedlings will come up year after year. Choose one of the compact varieties in white, pink, lilac or violet.

Anchusa. A very useful mound-forming annual for the border or containers is the dwarf *Anchusa* Blue Angel with showy heads of ultramarine-blue flowers, borne over a long period in summer. It is about 9 in (23 cm) tall.

Bartonia. A splendid way of introducing bright yellow into the border over a long period in summer is with *B. aurea*, 1½ ft (45 cm) tall, and with flowers not unlike those of hypericum (St John's wort).

Burning Bush, see Kochia

Calendula (Pot Marigold). Probably the easiest to grow of all annuals and even more likely than alyssum to become a permanent occupant of the garden. Unfortunately self-sown seedlings usually deteriorate in quality rapidly, and it is wise to pull them out and renew each year from purchased seed. There are many good varieties ranging in height from 1 to 2 ft (30 to 60 cm) and in colour from cream through the yellows to orange.

Candytuft, see Iberis

Centaurea cyanus (Cornflower). The taller cornflowers, which may reach a height of 3 ft (1 m), are excellent for cutting but not very serviceable in the border, for which purpose the dwarf kinds in blue, white or mixed colours are the most suitable.

Centaurea moschata (Sweet Sultan). The scented feathery flowers in a range of colours – yellow, white, pink through mauve to purple – make this a most decorative plant for a sunny position. There are mixed varieties available which grow to a height of 1½ ft (45 cm).

Chrysanthemum. The annual chrysanthemums are not to be confused with the perennial kinds grown in the border and greenhouse. Those grown nowadays are derived from the tricolor chrysanthemum (*C. carinatum*), most of which have a band of deep colour dividing the central yellow disc from the lighter colour outside, and the garland chrysanthemum (*C. coronarium*), which have either single or double flowers in self colours. Most are between 1½ and 2 ft (45 and 60 cm) high. Beautiful colour combinations are found in the Tricolor strain Catherine Wheels – from orange and scarlet to rose and

pink – and in Tricolor Mixed. Golden Gem is a good double variety of the *coronarium* type. There are also crosses between the two types with heights of 2½ to 4 ft (75 cm to 1·25 m).

Clarkia. A good many hardy annuals produce their flowers in flat heads. Clarkias, by contrast, carry their flowers in narrow spikes which make a useful contrast in form. They also have a fine range of colour from white through pale pink and salmon-rose, to carmine and crimson. Named varieties are listed by some seed firms but usually mixtures are offered.

Clary. Botanically known as *Salvia horminum* this plant is easily grown and carries tiers of pink, mauve, purple or white bracts on 2-ft (60-cm) stems. Sown from March to May where it is to grow, it produces an abundance of colourful flowering stems which can be used in summer flower arrangements or dried for winter decoration.

Convolvulus. The annual varieties of convolvulus bring some of the richest shades of blue and purple into the garden. They succeed in the worst of soil given plenty of sunshine. The variety of *C. minor* widely grown is Royal Ensign with wedgwood-blue flowers, 1 ft (30 cm) tall, while another of half that height coming rapidly to the fore is the dwarf Blue Flash, a rich blue contrasted by white and yellow in the centre of the flower. This

Ornamental grasses show off well the bright colours of annuals. Here, *Hordeum jubatum* (squirrel tail grass) blends well with the pink and white *Godetia* Sybil Sherwood and *Dimorphotheca* Giant Orange

last is ideal for use in window boxes and other containers as well as for the border.

Coreopsis. The annual varieties of coreopsis are still sometimes listed in catalogues under their obsolete botanical name *Calliopsis*. They are daisy flowers usually in shades of yellow with crimson or maroon. Separate colours can be purchased under varietal names, but this is another flower I like to see in mixture. The plants grow 2 to 2½ ft (60 to 75 cm) high and will need the support of twiggy branches.

Cornflower, see Centaurea cyanus

Cynoglossum. The superb blue forget-me-not-like flowers of cynoglossum are produced in abundance on rough upright stems carried above downy foliage. This plant is an ideal ground-cover subject for semi-shade and will reach a height of 18 in (45 cm).

Delphinium, Annual (Larkspur). The larkspurs are delphiniums but in gardens the name has been confined almost entirely to the annual varieties, delphinium being reserved for the perennials. The annuals are lovely flowers with long slender spikes of bloom, and a wonderful colour range from white through palest lavender and

Centaurea **Polka Dot is a bushy, dwarf cornflower suitable for massing at the front of a border. The flowers, of mixed colours, are carried on 1-ft (30-cm) stems. Cornflowers are ideal for cottage gardens**

The annual delphinium (or larkspur) is available in colours from white to pink, crimson and deep blue. Here it is flanked by *Helianthus* Dwarf Sungold and lavatera and backed by amaranthus (love lies bleeding)

pink to violet and crimson. The very finest flowers are obtained by sowing in early autumn, but good results can also be had from a spring sowing.

This is another flower where mixtures are usually offered nowadays like the Stock Flowered and Dwarf Hyacinth Flowered, the last only 1 ft (30 cm) tall against the Stock-flowered strain's 3 ft (1 m). The Giant Imperial strain is still very much available in mixture or in named varieties.

Eschscholzia. This is another annual inclined to take charge of the garden if you allow it to and one that, like the calendula, will then decline in quality very rapidly. Modern strains have a wonderful colour range from white and pale yellow to orange and crimson, amber, pink and rose. Good mixtures of both singles and doubles can be obtained, as well as individual colours in varying heights.

Godetia. There are two distinct types of godetia, the Azalea-flowered or Whitneyi varieties which make compact, freely branched plants 12 to 18 in (30 to 45 cm) high, and the varieties derived from *G. amoena* which carry their flowers in spikes 2 ft (60 cm) or more in height. I think for display in the garden the Azalea-flowered varieties are the more desirable. First-class mixtures can be obtained giving a range of colour from white through all shades of pink to crimson, but this is an annual that looks well in blocks of a colour.

Gypsophila. The annual gypsophilas are derived from *G. elegans*, a species which has now been developed to produce a rose-pink strain as well as the customary white varieties. The delicate airy flowers are produced in cascades on 18-in (45-cm) stems.

Helianthus. The ever-remarkable common sunflower, *H. annuus*, which is capable of lifting its yellow flowers to a considerable height and in consequence requires a position at the back of the border. There are several smaller forms which are of more manageable proportions and produce flowers in creamy-white, bronze and red as well as yellow. Especially effective is the completely double Dwarf Sungold.

Helichrysum. Of particular value for cutting and drying for winter decoration, the annual helichrysums are easily grown. Heights vary from 18 in to 3 ft (45 cm to 1 m) and colours from white to yellow, orange, deep pink and rich brown. The flowers, which are crisp and shiny, are best if cut before they are fully open and then hung upside down in a dry place.

Iberis (Candytuft). The flowers are produced in flattish heads in the common candytuft and in fat spikes in the Giant-flowered or rocket candytuft. The rocket candytuft is white but the common candytuft has a good range of colour from white to crimson. The dwarf Fairy Mixed strain is excellent for bedding out with a height of 8 in to 9 in (20 to 23 cm) and colours from red, through pink and lavender to white, while, among named varieties, the slightly taller Red Flash – a striking carmine-red shade – stands out.

Kochia (Burning Bush, Summer Cypress). A pleasing foil for other brightly coloured plants, the feathery foliage of the summer cypress, or burning bush, turns from rich mid-green to copper as the temperature falls at the end of the summer. It grows rapidly into a bush some 2 or 3 ft (60 cm to 1 m) high and 1 ft (30 cm) across.

Larkspur, see Delphinium

Lathyrus odoratus (Sweet Pea). The ordinary sweet peas can be used as a background to the border where they can be grown naturally without stopping or removing the side shoots. Alternatively, groups of them can be used to form columns of colour at the back of the border. However, the possibilities with sweet peas have now been greatly increased by the introduction of really good dwarf varieties, such as Early Dwarf Bijou Mixed, which only grows 1 ft (30 cm) high and has an excellent colour range, and the splendid Jet Set strain which, in recent years, has made a name for itself.

These Jet Set sweet peas combine a height of only 3 ft (1 m) with the quality of bloom associated with the Spencer-type sweet peas, the colours are excellent and

they make an admirable low hedge within the garden if such is needed.

Lavatera. This is one of the larger annuals making big bushy plants 2 or 3 ft (60 cm to 1 m) in height and as much through, but with stems so sturdy that they are well able to support themselves. The finest variety is Loveliness with large mallow-like flowers of a gleaming rose colour, and this is now joined by some taller varieties which grow up to 4 ft (1·25 m).

Limnanthes douglasii. This is a flower of considerable charm with its spreading habit and white and yellow flowers. It is excellent for edging paths and sprawling over steps, not growing over 6 in (15 cm) tall. A rather moist soil is preferred.

Love-in-a-Mist, see Nigella

Marigold, Pot, see Calendula

Mignonette, see Reseda

Nasturtium, see Tropaeolum

Nigella. This is the love-in-a-mist, so called because the flowers, typically blue and a little like cornflowers, are carried in a haze of the fine fern-like leaves. A delightful variety is the deep blue Miss Jekyll, and other colours like pink, rose, mauve, purple, and white are present in mixed varieties.

Pansy. Sown in boxes in a cold frame from May to July and planted out where they are to flower in September and October, pansies will provide a welcome show of colour throughout the winter months and on into the spring. The range of colours is now very wide, with the popular white, yellow, blue and mauve kinds now being joined by flame and scarlet varieties. All are no more than 9 in (23 cm) high and will thrive in most soils.

Papaver. The Shirley and Paeony-flowered poppies are the two most widely grown kinds; the former being available in both single and double forms, and the latter only in its characteristic large, double-flowered strains. All bear vibrantly colourful flowers of red, yellow, orange, pink and white, many with contrasting dark blue stamens. The Shirley poppies are 2 ft (60 cm) high and the Paeony-flowered 3 ft (1 m) high.

Phacelia. Another of the outstanding blue annuals, *P. campanularia* is a low-growing carpeter with bell-shaped rich gentian-blue flowers which can be had in bloom some six weeks from seed sowing. A taller (1½-ft, 45-cm) variety is the deep blue Blue Bonnet. Give them a sunny place.

When something tall and bold is required for the back of a border, remember the sunflowers. *Helianthus annuus* grows to 6 or 8 ft (2 to 2·5 m) but varieties are available from 2 ft (60 cm) high in many colours

Pincushion Flower, see Scabiosa

Poppy, see Papaver

Reseda odorata (Mignonette). This is not a showy annual but the creamy-white flowers are deliciously fragrant and it has the merit of associating well with any of the bright colours to be found in the annual border and helping to break them up. Mignonette does best in a soil that contains some lime. There are several named varieties with flowers in shades of red and yellow.

Scabiosa. The pincushion flower is, perhaps, best known in its perennial varieties, but the kinds grown as annuals extend the colour range from blue, pink and white to encompass dark pink, red and mauve in both single- and double-flowered forms. The flowers are produced on 15-in to 3-ft (38-cm to 1-m) stems.

Summer Cypress, see Kochia

Sunflower, see Helianthus

Sweet Alyssum, see Alyssum

Sweet Pea, see Lathyrus

Sweet Sultan, see Centaurea moschata

Tropaeolum (Nasturtium). The old-fashioned nasturtiums that ramble all over the place are not much use in the modern garden except to form a quick screen over unsightly objects. For the annual border the various dwarf or Tom Thumb nasturtiums are the ones to grow. Many have double or semi-double flowers in brilliant yellows, oranges and reds. The mixture called Dwarf Jewel Mixed has flowers in many different colours.

Very popular now, too, is the Whirlybird strain with spur-less flowers which is available in mixture or in individual colours.

Half-hardy Annuals

Ageratum. First-rate plants to edge a border or provide the groundwork beneath taller flowers. They give an altogether softer effect than lobelia. Some varieties grow only 4 in (10 cm) high, but others grow from 6 to 8 in (15 to 20 cm) high. Colours include a good range of blues, together with pink, reddish-mauve and white.

Antirrhinum (Snapdragon). These are excellent flowers for providing colour the summer through, especially the low-growing (9- to 15-in [23- to 38-cm] high) Tom Thumb varieties which can be used effectively in containers. Then there are the intermediate varieties (15 to 18 in [38 to 45 cm] tall) which are also very useful for bedding, and the tall varieties (3 ft [1 m]) which are as good for cutting as for border display. Rust can be a problem with antirrhinums and where this is the case it is advisable to grow the rust-resistant varieties.

Aster. This is another flower to provide colour the summer through and there is an excellent colour range, like the antirrhinums referred to above. Red, pink, yellow, blue, mauve, and white are found here. The flower styles vary greatly, too, from dwarf varieties (6 to 12 in [15 to 30 cm] tall) with semi-double or double flowers, to the 2-ft (60-cm) tall, rounded Powder-puffs mixture and the shaggy-flowered Ostrich Plume varieties, some 18 in (45 cm) tall. Of particular interest is the dwarf mixed strain, 8 in (20 cm) high, whose double ball-like flowers have a splended colour range in blue, red, pink, white and pale yellow.

Calceolaria. Brilliantly coloured half-hardy annuals with yellow, red, orange and brown pouch-like flowers which are frequently mottled with darker or lighter spots. Many hybrid strains are available, ranging in height from 8 to 15 in (20 to 38 cm).

Carnation. Treated as half-hardy annuals, some of the perennial strains of carnation bring the added attraction of scent to the annual border. The Chabaud and Enfant de Nice varieties are amongst the most popular; they are 18 in (45 cm) high with white, pink and red double flowers. Other dwarf strains are available which are only 9 in (23 cm) high, some of them flowering earlier than the Chabaud types and being equally strongly scented.

Dahlia. Though strictly speaking they are perennials, the Coltness Hybrid dahlias are usually treated as half-hardy annuals, being sown under glass from February to April and planted out in May to flower later in the summer. Apart from these 18-in (45-cm) hybrids, many strains are available in a wide variety of colours in both single- and double-flowered forms, ranging in height from 9 in to 4 ft (23 cm to 1·25 m).

Dianthus. The pinks grown as annuals are hybrids derived mainly from *D. heddewigii* and *D. chinensis* and range in height from 4 to 15 in (10 to 38 cm). They provide a rich variety of colours ranging from pure white through pink to bright red, many of them being bicoloured and some of them being deliciously scented.

Dimorphotheca. This delightful South African annual brings a whole range of unusual colours to the garden. A good mixture of *D. aurantiaca* will cover buff, apricot, salmon and orange. Alternatively, separate colours can be purchased.

Felicia. The kingfisher daisy, *F. bergeriana*, is a good subject for a sunny spot at the front of a border. Sow under glass from February to April and plant out in late May. The pale blue flowers with a yellow centre are produced on 6-in (15-cm) stems throughout the summer months.

Livingstone Daisy, see Mesembryanthemum

Lobelia. Strictly speaking a half-hardy perennial, but

lobelia is almost invariably grown as a half-hardy annual and so I include it here. It is, with alyssum and ageratum, the most popular of all edging and groundwork plants, but choose a lobelia that really is compact in habit. String of Pearls is a mixture of colours including white, pink, blue and violet.

Marigold, French and African, see Tagetes

Mesembryanthemum. Most mesembryanthemums are perennials but the Livingstone daisy, *M. criniflorum*, is a splendidly colourful half-hardy annual with daisy-like flowers in a wide range of colours of exceptional brilliance. It sprawls flat on the ground and makes an admirable carpet or edging, but its flowers only open in sunshine, so face it south if possible.

Nemesia. The lovely varieties of *N. strumosa* cover a cheerful range of colours. They look wonderful in mixture or in blocks of one colour. Choose good compact varieties such as Blue Gem, Fire King, scarlet, and Carnival Mixture.

Nicotiana (Tobacco Plant). The fragrant tobacco plants, varieties of *N. affinis*, are comparatively tall on the whole (2 to 3 ft [60 cm to 1 m]), but there are dwarf varieties of only 10 in (25 cm).

They differ from many annuals in that they will grow well in partly shaded places, and while the usual practice is for the flowers to open in the evening only there are numerous varieties and strains now which have flowers which are open all day. The colour range is wide – crimson, pink, white and an unusual but attractive greenish yellow.

Penstemon. These are valuable plants for the back or centre of a border, producing 3-ft (1-m) spires of flowers ranging in colour from white, pink, rose and lavender blue to pure magenta, many of the darker colours being mottled in the throat with white. Though strictly

The fluffy seed heads of *Lagurus ovatus*, the hare's tail grass, pierce this mound of cerise petunias and lead the eye to other plantings. The rich green of a well-kept lawn shows off all the colours to advantage

This arrangement of fragrant nicotianas, petunias in many brilliant shades and hanging baskets of fuchsias shows what can be done to brighten a shady corner

perennials, they are treated as half-hardy annuals. The Monarch Strain is particularly popular.

Petunia. These are quickly becoming the most popular of summer-bedding plants, and have been developed so rapidly by breeders that the number of varieties available is now bewildering. For garden display the varieties with medium-sized blooms are best, but the large petunias and double-flowered varieties look well in ornamental vases, window-boxes and so on. Wonderful, intense colours are available, such as magenta, pink, violet, red, crimson, blue and white.

Phlox. Individually the flowers of the annual phlox are not unlike those of the perennial phlox, but the habit of the plants is quite different as the stems are thin and they trail along the ground producing a jewelled mosaic of brilliantly coloured flowers. The colour range is from white to crimson and violet with some light yellows and buffs but no strong yellows.

Pinks, see Dianthus

Portulaca. For sunny positions in well-drained, light soil in borders as well as the rock garden the colourful, 6-in (15-cm) tall portulacas are a splendid choice. Both double- and single-flowered strains are available in a colour range which includes purple, shades of orange, red, yellow, purple and white.

Rudbeckia. This was an annual that did not attract much attention until the introduction of the large-flowered tetraploid varieties now sold as gloriosa daisies. These make big plants 3 to 4 ft (1 to 1·25 m) high with large, very showy, daisy-like flowers in various shades of yellow, orange, mahogany-red and bronze. There are both single-flowered and double-flowered strains. But the real advance here has been the arrival of the superb Rustic Dwarfs – 1½ ft (45 cm) tall or a little more, with the most lovely colouring of gold, bronze, red and mahogany surrounding a central core of purplish black.

Salvia. The strains of *S. splendens* are excellent bedding plants with scarlet, pink or violet flower spikes splashed, in some instances, with white. Most strains are 12 in (30 cm) high and form rounded plants which carry their flower spikes in profusion until the first frosts of autumn.

Snapdragon, see Antirrhinum

Stock. A long flowering season coupled with a powerful fragrance makes the Ten-week stocks a valuable addition to the garden. Flowers are produced on 1- to 2-ft (30- to 60-cm) spikes in colours ranging from white through light and dark pink to magenta.

Tagetes (Marigold). In America the marigold is one of the most popular of all summer flowers and it has gained much in popularity in Britain thanks to the introduction of fine new varieties. The range of form is quite astonishing, from miniatures such as the dwarf African marigolds and the Petite strain of French marigolds, to things like the giant African varieties, 1½ to 3 ft (45 cm to 1 m) tall with large flowers. For garden display, though, some of the medium-height marigolds take a lot of beating and blend in better than the big mop heads; for instance, varieties of the dwarf French single type in brilliant yellows and reds and ranging from 6 to 12 in (15 to 30 cm) in height. For edging, too, there is the single, orange-flowered, 6-in (15-cm) tall *T. signata pumila* and its varieties.

Tobacco Plant, see Nicotiana

Zinnia. Given plenty of sunshine how lovely the zinnias can be in the summer border, and how useful for cutting for the home! Big advances have been made in these flowers with the introduction of fine F_1 hybrids in scarlet and pink, growing to a height of 2 ft (60 cm), and the dwarf F_1 hybrids which grow to only half that height and come in an excellent range of colours.

Then, of course, there are tall zinnias like the giant Dahlia-flowered strain 2½ ft (75 cm), and the quilled-petal strain with flowers like chrysanthemums – an interesting genus, given the right weather.

Annuals are of great value in prolonging the flowering season of an herbaceous border and provide filling material for unsightly gaps. This mixture of half-hardy annuals and herbaceous perennials includes salvias, nemesias, French marigolds, alyssum, lobelia and phlox

Concerning Hardy Plants

Hardy plants or herbaceous perennials, whichever you prefer to call them, are the backbone of a great many gardens. Unlike annuals and bedding plants, they will go on for years without renewal or disturbance, though this is not the best way to grow many of them. Some, such as peonies, Japanese anemones and hellebores, positively dislike being moved but they are in a minority. Most hardy plants benefit from being lifted and divided every third or fourth year. Michaelmas daisies produce their finest flowers when lifted and divided annually.

Few hardy plants are fussy about soil. Some, such as pyrethrums, gaillardias and geraniums, dislike heavy, badly drained soil and the leaves of lupins may be yellow where there is much chalk or lime. But in general if the soil is well broken up with a spade or fork and given a scattering of a good all-purpose fertilizer, hardy plants will grow and flower freely.

The taller kinds may need quite a lot of staking but hardy plants up to about 3 ft (1 m) tall will either stand up on their own, or find all the support they require from a few short hazel stems or other twiggy branches pushed in around them in spring, so that the stems grow through the sticks and conceal them.

Perhaps the most important development, though, in this area is the much more imaginative use we make nowadays of these fascinating plants. Not only are they superbly displayed in island beds, with the great advantage to the viewer that the plants can be enjoyed from every angle, but such a feature provides infinite scope for creating interesting shapes suited to the garden.

In addition, herbaceous perennials are now invariably mixed in with annuals and shrubs to provide greater diversity of interest over a long period and, in small gardens, widen in every possible way the options open to the gardener. Such mixed borders can be a joy.

Indeed, the shapes found in perennial flowers provide many opportunities for imaginative displays, whether it is the bold flat flower heads of plants like the achilleas Gold Plate and Coronation Gold or the sedums Autumn Joy and Brilliant; lovely poker flowers such as are found in polygonums like *P. bistorta superbum* and the red hot pokers (kniphofias); or flamboyant daisy flowers perhaps best characterized by the rudbeckias and heleniums. What good use can be found, too, in a colour sense, for the airy haze created by the flowers of *Thalictrum dipterocarpum* Hewitt's Double and *Heucherella tiarelloides*, which, like all the others mentioned here, are described on the pages which follow.

Nor should one overlook those many perennials which have excellent flowers and unusually good foliage, invariably of the greatest possible value for providing efficient ground cover. I'm thinking particularly of things like the hostas (plantain lilies), bergenias, the *Polygonum affine* varieties Donald Lowndes and Darjeeling Red, geums, ajugas (bugles) and lamiums. Some of these are strongly coloured, more of them fairly restrained in tone, but all can be infinitely satisfying if carefully integrated into the garden scene. Again there is more about them and the conditions they need in the pages which follow and on pp. 111 to 117.

Some Easy Kinds

Here are some good easy kinds with which to begin:

Acanthus. Plants with real architectural value are always an asset to the garden and *A. mollis latifolius* is no exception. The bold foliage is thistle like and the heads of white and purple flowers, borne in late summer, have a foxglove-like appearance. It is, moreover, an adaptable plant succeeding in sun or shade, although preferring sunny conditions, and a moist soil.

Achillea (Yarrow). I have already stressed the importance of white flowers to break up the strong colours without dulling them (see p. 13). For this purpose *Achillea* The Pearl is in the first rank as its small double white flowers are freely produced from June to August on plants 2 to 3 ft (60 cm to 1 m) high that need little or no staking. A. Coronation Gold has flat heads of yellow flowers over grey ferny leaves from June to September. A. *taygetea* and Moonshine repeat this in sulphur yellow, but do not flower for so long.

For spectacle, though, plant either A. *filipendulina* Gold Plate or the smaller Coronation Gold, both have the very showy plate-like flowers of strong golden-yellow which add strength to any bed or border. Gold Plate is around 5 ft (1.5 m) tall and July and August flowering, while Coronation Gold is 3 ft (1 m) tall – an ideal height for many situations – and in flower right through from June to September.

Aconitum (Monkshood). The monkshoods are fine plants though not widely grown perhaps because they are poisonous – but for that matter so are Christmas roses and lilies-of-the-valley. However, there are not so many blue spike-flowered perennials that we can afford to neglect any as good as these. One of the best, because it needs little or no staking, is Bressingham Spire, 3 ft (1 m) high, violet-blue and flowering in July and August. Another freely available is Blue Sceptre, 2 ft (60 cm), with a similar flowering period. These and other aconitums grow well in sun or shade.

Agapanthus. The *Agapanthus* Headbourne Hybrids are superb border plants and hardier than any of their relatives, which have a reputation for tenderness and are more often grown as tub plants for overwintering in the cool greenhouse or for growing permanently under glass.

The Headbourne Hybrids, with flowers in all shades from light to dark blue, do well out of doors in sunny sheltered borders in many parts of the country. The lily-like flowers are borne in impressive heads on 3-ft (1-m) stems above strap-shaped leaves. Good soil drainage is essential.

Ajuga. The A. *reptans* varieties which grow well in sunshine or light shade are superb ground coverers. One of the best is *multicolor* with leaves variegated in bronze, pink and cream; a recent introduction, Burgundy Glow, has leaves in a mixture of green, cream and magenta. A mass of rich blue flower spikes rise from the mat-like surface in early summer.

Anchusa (Alkanet). For early blue in the middle and back of the border A. *italica* is the one to choose in one or other of its numerous varieties, such as Loddon Royalist, 3 ft (1 m) gentian blue; Morning Glory, 5 ft (1.5 m) dark blue; and Opal, 4 ft (1.25 m) light blue. All bloom in late May or June. They like sunshine and well-drained soil.

A traditional herbaceous border planted at the foot of a high wall. The wall acts as a muted background for the flowers, and climbers can be trained against it to provide more colour and increase its effectiveness

Two popular hardy perennial plants in contrasting colours are shown here together. The flat yellow heads of achillea tower above the purple-blue spires of nepeta and give height to this rather wide herbaceous border

Anemone (Windflower). The Japanese anemones (varieties of *A. hybrida*, quite often listed incorrectly as *A. japonica*) are valuable for their late flowering in August and September when their saucer-shaped flowers in white, pink or rose make a pleasant change from the prevailing Michaelmas daisies. Heights vary from 2 ft to 4 ft (60 cm to 1·25 m). Good varieties include the semi-double white, Louise Uhink, 3½ ft (1·15 m); Whirlwind, 4 ft (1·25 m), also white; the delightful pink September Charm, 2 ft (60 cm); and Profusion, another pink, also 2 ft (60 cm) tall.

Artemisia. Most of the artemisias are shrubs, but *A. lactiflora* is a fine herbaceous plant, 5 ft (1·5 m) tall with elegant plumy sprays of small white flowers in August and September. It is another of those whites so useful for breaking up the strong colours. Grow in a sunny position.

Aster (Michaelmas Daisies). All the host of Michaelmas daisies must be considered here, starting in August with the bushy *amellus* varieties, of which the single blue King George, 2 ft (60 cm), is still the most popular, and finishing up with the bewilderingly numerous varieties of *novi-belgii*, like the double, blue Marie Ballard, pale pink Apple Blossom and Winston S. Churchill, beetroot red. Most of these are 3 or 4 ft (1 to 1·25 m) high and need some staking and fairly frequent division, too, if they are not to get untidy. But there are also dwarf varieties such as the lilac-mauve Audrey, 15 in (38 cm), the rich blue Lady in Blue, 10 in (25 cm) and the cerise Jenny, 12 in (30 cm).

Astilbe. These are the plants often called spiraea, with plume-like sprays of flowers in July and August. They dislike hot, dry places. Heights are mostly around 2½ to 3 ft (75 cm to 1 m), except for the varieties of *A. simplicifolia* which are 1 ft (30 cm) or less. Good varieties of normal height are Bressingham Beauty and Rhineland, pink; Federsee, rosy red; and Irrlicht, white, while perhaps the best known of all is the striking rich red Fanal.

The most important need of astilbes is a good deep soil which is reasonably moisture retentive although well drained. Once settled they should be left alone until a deterioration of performance indicates the need for division and replanting. Do this in spring or autumn.

Bee Balm, see Monarda

Bergamot, see Monarda

Bergenia. These large-leaved ground coverers, which used to be known as megaseas and saxifragas, are splendid garden plants of very easy cultivation, although not everybody would agree, perhaps, on the attractions

This border, seen at the height of summer, has been well planned to give a combination of contrasting colours and heights. The spiky blue veronica shows off the pink of the phlox to advantage, being backed itself by the tall, yellow, plate-like flowers of achillea

Although only 1 ft (30 cm) high, *Campanula glomerata dahurica* is a stately plant. It likes a sunny position at the front of a border and flowers in June and July

of the glossy leathery foliage. Perhaps the best position of all for them is beside a pool or a path, but wherever they are grown their bold spikes of flowers are certain to be enjoyed in March and April. The species commonly grown is the 1-ft (30-cm) tall *B. cordifolia*, but two varieties of special worth are Ballawley, with rose-red flowers and a little later flowering, and *schmidtii*, pink flowered and early, with especially attractive broad leaves.

Campanula. Many of the campanulas are rock garden plants but there are big herbaceous kinds, too, one of the tallest being *C. lactiflora*, 5 ft (1·5 m), with loose clusters of light blue cup-shaped flowers in July and August. Loddon Anna is a mauve-pink counterpart and Pouffe a pale blue, remarkable cushion-like variety only a foot (30 cm) high. In the intermediate height range, 2 to 3 ft (75 cm to 1 m), the varieties of *C. persicifolia*, blue or white and sometimes double-flowered, are useful for colour in the first half of summer. *C. persicifolia* Telham Beauty, with single china-blue flowers is lovely. For June–July flowering there is the purple-violet *C. latifolia* Brantwood. *C. glomerata dahurica* is a splendid violet-purple species with flowers in June and July tightly clustered on 1-ft (30-cm) stems. All grow well in a wide range of soils in open, sunny situations but *lactiflora* varieties will also do well in light shade.

Catmint, see Nepeta

Chinese Balloon Flower, see Platycodon

Chrysanthemum. In addition to the annual chrysanthemums and the florist chrysanthemums there are hardy border varieties often called shasta daisies or moon daisies. All are white, 2 to 3 ft (60 cm to 1 m) high and July–August flowering. Everest is a very well-known single variety; while Esther Read and Wirral Supreme are fine examples of varieties with double flowers; Christine Hagemann is one of the varieties with semi-double flowers, and Thomas Killin one of the anemone-flowered type. All make solid areas of white in summer.

Coneflower, see Rudbeckia

Coreopsis. These very strong and undemanding plants ask only for good drainage and plenty of sunshine to do well. *C. verticillata grandiflora*, only 2 ft (60 cm) high, is one of the finest of all perennials for the front of the border, carrying its rich yellow flowers from July to September. Goldfink, deep yellow and also with a long period of flowering is a true dwarf only 9 in (23 cm) tall, while Badengold is taller (3 ft [1 m]) with showy golden-yellow flowers.

Day Lily, see Hemerocallis

Delphinium. The delphiniums are the noblest and in some ways the most exciting of all herbaceous plants but they do need a little more management than most – careful staking, proper feeding, fairly frequent renewal from cuttings or seeds. There are first-rate seed strains such as the Pacific Giants giving a wide range of colours, including white, lilac-pink, lavender, light blue, dark blue and purple. There are also a great many named varieties such as the cornflower-blue Ann Page; the purple Royal Marine; silvery mauve Silver Moon; and Icecap, pure white. The modern varieties mostly fall in the $5\frac{1}{2}$- to $6\frac{1}{2}$-ft (1·5- to 2·15-m) height range, a few reaching 7 ft (2·25 m), but there are also shorter varieties of between 3 to 4 ft (1 to 1·25 m). Then, of course, there are the very pretty Belladonna varieties which branch freely and carry their flowers in sprays rather than in spikes. These are usually about 4 ft (1·25 m) high. Wendy, gentian blue, and Blue Bees, light blue, are typical.

Echinops (Globe Thistle). Known as the globe thistle because of the spiky globular heads of blue or white flowers. Taplow Blue with dark blue flowers is one of the best. It grows 5 ft (1·5 m) tall. *E. ritro* is smaller, around 3 ft (1 m). Both bring a distinctive element to the border and are best planted in deeply dug ground to allow their tap roots to delve down. They are excellent cut flowers as well.

Erigeron. These look like Michaelmas daisies but are

These formal double borders have been planted with predominantly blue flowers which create a peaceful atmosphere. The closely clipped tree acts as an elegant focal point at the end of the short vista

quite short and flower from June to August, some to September. Good varieties are Darkest of All, 2 ft (60 cm), deep deep blue; Charity, 2½ ft (75 cm), pale pink; Foerster's Liebling, 1½ ft (45 cm), a semi-double-flowered rose-pink; and Dignity, 1½ ft (45 cm) violet.

Eryngium (Sea Holly). These are the sea hollies, with teazle-like flower heads surrounded by ruffs of stiff bracts, which in some varieties are finely cut and attractively coloured. Like the globe thistles they are welcome because they are so different. Two good kinds are *E. tripartitum*, 3 ft (1 m), with many small metallic blue flowers and *E. bourgatii*, silvery-blue and only half that height. Both bloom from June to August and are very showy.

Gaillardia. Few perennials are capable of making so concentrated a display for two or three months, roughly from midsummer to late August. The plants do, however, tend to wear themselves out and should be renewed fairly frequently from seed or root cuttings. Good varieties are Ipswich Beauty, deep yellow and red; Mandarin, orange-flame; Wirral Flame, reddish-bronze; and Goblin, red and yellow. All grow about 2½ to 3 ft (75 cm to 1 m) high, except Goblin which is only about 9 in (23 cm) tall, and need bushy twigs for support. They like sunny places and well-drained rather poor soil.

Geranium. Not to be confused with our old friends the pelargoniums, these are the herbaceous plants which have geranium as their Latin generic name. One of the finest of these easily pleased ground-covering plants for colour is *G. psilostemon* with magenta-red, black-centred flowers in early summer; another, the very low-growing *G. sanguineum lancastriense splendens,* only 6 in (15 cm) tall, which bears a mass of rose-pink flowers from early summer until August. Another excellent variety is *G. wallichianum* Buxton's Variety, a lovely deep blue for colour in the second half of summer. But there are many more, mostly as happy in light shade as in sunshine, although *G. s. lancastriense splendens* does need sun. Any well-drained soil will suit them.

Geum. That familiar flower the geum is always a source of pleasure in the second half of summer. It does best in poorish soil with full sun and good drainage. Mrs Bradshaw, scarlet, and Lady Stratheden, yellow, are the best known varieties – both around 2 ft (60 cm) tall – while another of note is the orange-red Fire Opal, slightly shorter.

Globe Flower, see Trollius

Globe Thistle, see Echinops

Golden Rod, see Solidago

Phlox are particularly long-lasting border flowers which vary in height from 1 ft (30 cm) or so to about 4 ft (1·25 m) and in colour from white and pink to magenta, crimson and blue, many with contrasting 'eyes'

Gypsophila. These are useful for their lightness and elegance. The flowers are small but produced with the utmost freedom in loose cloudy sprays. One of the best is Bristol Fairy with double white flowers. It grows 3 ft (1 m) tall. Flamingo repeats this in lilac-pink; Rosy Veil is also pink but only 1 ft (30 cm) tall. All flower from July to September.

Helenium. Useful because they give solid masses of yellow, bronze and crimson from mid- to late summer and suitable for growing in any reasonable soil in sunshine or light shade. Good varieties are Butterpat, yellow, 3 ft (1 m), very late flowering; Wyndley, coppery-orange, 2 ft (60 cm); and Moerheim Beauty, wallflower red, 3 ft (1 m).

Helianthus (Sunflower). These are the perennial sunflowers and many of them are too tall or too invasive for the ordinary garden. The variety which can be recommended is Loddon Gold with large, double golden-yellow flowers in July and August. It grows 5 ft (1·5 m) tall and is very easy to please given good drainage and sunshine.

Heliopsis. The effect is similar to that of the perennial sunflowers but there are some even richer shades of yellow, and in the later part of summer and early autumn their colour is welcome. Varieties include Orange King, 5 ft (1·5 m), and the 4-ft (1·25-m) Golden Plume. They have such stiff stems they need little support and the blooms are excellent for cutting.

Hemerocallis (Day Lily). These are known as day lilies because the trumpet-shaped flowers resemble lilies and each lasts for one day only. This is not such a drawback as it sounds as buds are freely produced and flowers open in rapid succession during July and August and some continue into September. The merits of the day lilies are that they are very easily grown in sunshine or light shade, while they require no staking and bring a different style of flower into the border. There are a great many varieties and the colour range has improved tremendously in recent years with everything from orange to red, pink, pale yellow and buff available in the varieties. Mostly, they are in the 2½- to 3-ft (75-cm to 1-m) height range. Pink Charm, Golden Chimes, Hyperion, yellow, Fandango, orange, are good varieties.

Heuchera. These very pretty flowers for the front of the border, in sunshine or light shade, are a delight in late spring and early summer when carrying their airy sprays of tiny flowers, but they are pleasing at other times, too, with their mat of good foliage. There are many varieties in shades of red and pink, even the odd one with whitish flowers, but there is a lot to be said for opting for the Bressingham Hybrids. These are 2 ft (60 cm) – the average height of nearly all heucheras.

Heucherella. *H. tiarelloides,* only 1 ft (30 cm) tall and a cross between *Heuchera brizoides* and *Tiarella cordifolia,* is another splendid choice for a bed in partial shade – a lovely sight from April to June when the graceful panicles of airy flowers are borne above the mat of rounded, shallowly lobed leaves. And even better is its slightly taller variety Bridget Bloom with light pink flowers.

Hosta (Plantain Lily). The plantain lilies are, of course, magnificent foliage plants but they also have attractive mauve or lavender-blue to white spikes of lily-like flowers in late summer, some continuing into early autumn. However, it is as foliage plants that we will include them here, picking out for special mention *H. crispula* whose wavy leaves in rich green have a cream edge, the bluish-grey leaved *H. sieboldiana*, very broad and patterned with corrugations, and *H. fortunei albopicta* which starts the season with its leaves yellow edged with green and, as the season progresses, turns completely green.

Hostas are ideal associates for shrubs, particularly the colourful rhododendrons and azaleas, but they also blend in beautifully with a very wide range of plants indeed. They grow well in sunshine or light shade, and are particularly useful for planting under the light shade of high-branched trees. They are very adaptable as to soil but if the ground can be dressed with well-rotted farmyard manure before planting, all to the good.

Iris. This marvellous family has one of its brightest stars in the May- to June-flowering tall bearded varieties, which I always feel are best planted in a bed of their own, rather than mixed with other herbaceous perennial plants. Still, that is a matter of opinion and it always has to be remembered that their flowering period is but a brief three weeks or so.

What they must have is sunshine and good soil drainage with the soil being given a good dressing of ground limestone. Good current varieties for colour – and the colours in this flower are exquisite – include the popular Jane Phillips, pale blue; Tarn Hows, cedarwood brown; Staten Island, bright yellow; June Meredith, deep pink; and Pinnacle, white and primrose yellow, which gives a hint of the wide colour range. All are around 2½ to 4 ft (75 cm to 1·25 m) tall.

Do not plant too deeply – the rhizomes should only be partly covered with soil, for they need to be ripened off by the sun after flowering finishes.

Then, for early-summer flowering for damp, but not stagnant, soil near the waterside or in borders generally, there are the lovely *I. sibirica* varieties in colours from purple to pale blue, almost grey; *I. kaempferi* and its varieties, and *I. laevigata* which is best actually growing in several inches of water.

For autumn display there is the gladwyn iris, *I. foetidissima*, which at that time produces flamboyant pods of brilliant scarlet seeds which persist into winter. And, best loved of all, there is the winter-flowering Algerian iris which we used to call *stylosa* and which is now *I. unguicularis*, a beautiful flower in shades of pale lavender blue (the colour depending on the form) which does best in a warm, sunny angle of a house wall in poor, well-drained soil. There are, of course, perennial irises of many other kinds, but these must suffice in the context of this book.

Kniphofia (Red Hot Poker and Torch Lily). These bring a highly distinctive flower shape to the border. The most familiar is *K. uvaria* with 4-ft (1·25-m) high red and yellow flower spikes in August and September. But you can start the season with Bee's Sunset, orange-red and 3 ft (1 m) tall, which begins to flower in June, continuing into July. Three splendid varieties for July and August are the scarlet and yellow Royal Standard, flame-red Samuel's Sensation and Jenny Bloom, salmon pink, all 3 ft (1 m) tall, while for flowering into autumn there is the variety C. M. Pritchard, a magnificent orangy shade. Despite their height none of these requires staking as the flower stems are thick and sturdy.

Very pretty indeed is the smaller, 1½-ft (45-cm) tall *K. galpinii* which bears orange-yellow flower spikes in September and October above grass-like foliage. Like all the other kniphofias it must have sunshine and first-rate soil drainage to do well.

Lupinus (Lupin). The splendid Russell lupins, some in self colours, others combining two contrasted colours in the same flower, need no recommendation as they are among the most popular perennials. Unfortunately they tend to be short lived and so should be fairly frequently renewed from seed or cuttings. Excellent seed strains are now available but these mostly give mixed colours.

Lychnis. For introducing brilliant red colour into the border between June and August few perennials can compete with the 3-ft (1-m) tall *L. chalcedonica*. Moreover, it is easily grown, given a free-draining soil.

Lythrum. The rather fierce magenta flower spikes need to be carefully placed in the garden but can be most effective. One of the best varieties is Robert, rosy-red. It is about 3 ft (1 m) tall and self-supporting.

Meadow Rue, see Thalictrum

Michaelmas Daisies, see Aster

Monarda. The bee balm or bergamot, *Monarda didyma*, is a plant for rather moist soils which canbe an asset the summer through with its rather ragged-looking flowers on 3-ft (1-m) stems. The varieties usually grown are Cambridge Scarlet and Croftway Pink.

Monkshood, see Aconitum

Moon Daisy, see Chrysanthemum

Nepeta (Catmint). The catmint, *N. faassenii*, is a popular edging plant because its grey foliage looks attractive and

The stately blooms of *Kniphofia* Royal Standard are held well clear of their grassy foliage to give a colourful display in July and August. The common names of red-hot pokers and torch lilies are well deserved

it flowers non-stop from June to September. The flowers are lavender blue and, in fact, the whole effect of this plant is comparable with that of lavender. It grows about 1 ft (30 cm) tall.

Paeonia (Peony). The peonies are the most opulent border flowers in May and June and are quite indispensable. Unfortunately they resent disturbance and often sulk for a year or so after being transplanted. Buy young plants in September, give them good rich soil and keep them well watered the first summer. There are innumerable varieties, none more showy than the Old Double Red and the single *P. lobata* (also known as *P. peregrina*). These, however, are not scented like the Chinese peonies such as Duchesse de Nemours, creamy-white; Sarah Bernhardt, rose; Solange, salmon; and Felix Crousse, red.

Papaver (Poppy). For the perennial border it is *P. orientale*, the Oriental poppy, that matters. From this you will certainly get Oriental splendour in scarlet, pink and white for a few weeks in late May and June, but a good deal of untidyness later. Try to mask this by planting something that will grow up in front of the poppies when they have faded. Marcus Perry, bright red; Goliath, crimson-red; Mrs Perry, salmon pink, and Perry's White are excellent varieties, all, except Mrs Perry (2½ ft, 75 cm), some 3 ft (1 m) tall.

Peony, see Paeonia

Phlox. The herbaceous phlox, like the peony in early summer, is quite indispensable in July, August and early September, both for solid masses of colour and fragrance. Good varieties are Brigadier, orange-red; Mia Ruys, white; Eventide, lavender; Border Gem, violet; and Otley Purple, but, of course, there are many more.

Physostegia. Some kinds are far too tall and straggly but not the obedient plant, *P. virginiana* Vivid. This is a first rate front-row plant with little 2-ft (60-cm) high spikes of bright rose flowers which come in September and October when they are especially welcome. The slightly taller, pure white variety Summer Snow flowers from July to September.

Plantain Lily, see Hosta

Platycodon (Chinese Balloon Flower). Aptly named the Chinese balloon flower because of the appearance of the swollen buds prior to opening, *P. grandiflorum mariesii* is a delight if you can provide it with the right conditions, namely a soil with plenty of body in it and good drainage. This variety is about 1 ft (30 cm) tall and the cup-shaped flowers open to an attractive palish blue colour.

Many of the herbaceous peonies (flowering in late May and June) are fully double but Lady Alexandra Duff is a semi-double which shows off to perfection the rich golden stamens

Polygonum. This very large family includes many invasive species which in the gardener's eyes are little better than weeds, but a relative few which are marvellous garden plants, especially in the ground-cover role. Such, for instance, as those two varieties of the low-growing, carpeting *P. affine* – Donald Lowndes, rose-pink, and the deeper pink Darjeeling Red. Neither exceeds 9 in (23 cm) in height and the pretty spikes of flowers are borne in summer over a long period.

Another especially useful polygonum is the quite different *P. bistorta superbum* which has large foliage and bears spikes of pink poker flowers on 2½-ft (75-cm) stems in the first half of summer. All these like moist soil and succeed in sun or light shade.

Poppy, see Papaver

Pyrethrum. If you can provide pyrethrums with a sunny home, reasonably light soil and good drainage then they will give a splendid return in the shape of masses of red, pink, salmon or white daisy flowers in May and June. The best known variety is the salmon-pink Eileen May Robinson, the next perhaps the white Avalanche. Other varieties of note include the pale pink Madeleine, and Brenda, cerise. All grow about 2½ ft (75 cm) tall and they are as useful for cutting as for garden display.

Red Hot Poker, see Kniphofia

Rudbeckia (Coneflower). Some of the perennial kinds are very tall plants that may blow over if not supported, but *Rudbeckia* Goldsturm suffers from no such drawback as it grows only 2½ ft (75 cm) high and has stiff wiry stems. The large daisy flowers are very showy, deep yellow with a black central disc and are around to be enjoyed from July to September. Give this plant a home in the sun, in any reasonably good soil.

Salvia. The best hardy salvia for a sunny position in the border is *S. superba*. Its narrow purple spikes are produced in great abundance in July and August. The common form grows 3 ft (1 m) tall but Lubeca is shorter, about 2 ft (60 cm), and East Friesland shorter still, only 1½ ft (45 cm).

Sea Holly, see Eryngium

Sedum (Stonecrop). Most of the stonecrops are rock plants but *S. spectabile* is a splendidly showy border plant for the front row. Its great flat heads of pink flowers attract butterflies, which add to their beauty. Brilliant is a deeper coloured variety. Both grow 1½ ft (45 cm) high and flower in August and September.

Two magnificent hybrids are Autumn Joy, 1½ ft (45 cm) tall, and Ruby Glow, 9 in (23 cm) tall, the latter bearing its rosy-red flower heads from July to early September and Autumn Joy its rosy-salmon flowers in September and October, the flowers deepening in colour as they mature.

Shasta Daisy, see Chrysanthemum

Sidalcea. The slender pink spikes of the sidalcea help to break up the more solid masses of colour in the border in the latter part of summer. There are a lot of varieties and not much difference between some of them but Rev. Page Roberts is soft pink, Rose Queen, rose-pink, and Croftway Red as near red as sidalceas get. All are about 4 ft (1.25 m) high and are perhaps best in sun although they will succeed in light shade.

Solidago (Golden Rod). These were once regarded as common and rather weedy flowers but they have now been made valuable by the introduction of short, bushy varieties such as Lemore, and Goldenmosa, all 2 or 3 ft (60 cm to 1 m) high with feathery masses of golden-yellow flowers in August and September.

Spiraea, see Astilbe

Stonecrop, see Sedum

Sunflower, see Helianthus

Thalictrum. The meadow rue, some 5 ft (1.5 m) tall, is a delightful border plant. The variety Hewitt's Double, with large branching panicles of lavender-lilac flowers, is the kind usually grown. The foliage is divided and fern like and makes another very attractive feature for the border.

Torch Lily, see Kniphofia

Trollius (Globe Flower). The trolliuses, or globe flowers, natural waterside plants, are some of the most colourful perennials for May to June colour with their gay orange or deep yellow flowers. They need a reasonably rich soil not lacking in moisture and delight in light shade. Good varieties are the orange-yellow Orange Princess; Golden Queen, of similar colouring to the last; Earliest of All, a palish yellow which is indeed early in coming into bloom; and Goldquelle, orange-yellow. All are around 2½ ft (75 cm) tall.

Veronica. The slender blue or pink spikes of the herbaceous veronicas are another of the antidotes to too much solidity in the border. Avoid the very tall varieties and go for those of short to medium height such as *V. longifolia* Foerster's Blue; *V. incana*, with grey leaves and deep blue flowers; and *V. spicata* Barcarolle, pink. These all flower in late summer, but the light blue, 2-ft (60-cm) tall *V. gentianoides*, flowers in May and June. This species also has a variegated form, *V. gentianoides variegata*, with richly marked leaves.

Windflower, see Anemone

Yarrow, see Achillea

In late May and June the Oriental poppies (papavers) are at their best. Colours range from the popular red with a black centre, to pink, salmon and white

Shrubs for Colour

The planning of a border of shrubs for colour does not present quite the same problems as one of herbaceous plants or annuals, except perhaps where rhododendrons and azaleas are to figure prominently, for their lavish colours, as already remarked (p. 14), can clash unless selected carefully. But with most shrubs the flowers are well balanced with green foliage which helps to avoid disharmony.

Shrubs can be had in flower in every month of the year and when planning a border they may be chosen to ensure the longest possible season of flower. Their form must also be taken into consideration, so that taller plants do not overcrowd those of dwarf habit, the lean and bony ones are balanced by those of more ample growth and foliage, and so on.

Special colour effects can also be created. It is possible to have gold and silver borders, making use of shrubs noted for their colourful foliage and stems as well as for their flowers. Heathers are very popular and their colours combine well with the foliage of conifers of various hues, especially the golden ones.

Everygreen shrubs are indispensable for the permanent colour effects they can create, and they also make splendid backgrounds to show up the flowers and foliage of other shrubs.

Colour Month by Month

JANUARY

Cornus (Dogwood). The moisture-loving dogwoods – they will also do well in soil less well served in terms of moisture – include kinds valuable for their colourful young stems in winter. Excellent kinds are the red-stemmed *C. alba sibirica*, of which there is also an attractive variegated form, *sibirica variegata*, and *C. stolonifera flaviramea*, which is yellow stemmed. These make shrubs 6 to 8 ft (2 to 2·5 m) tall and wide – the variegated-leaved form may be a little less – and hard pruning in spring will ensure a plentiful supply of the young growths which are the ones which provide the most colour.

Garrya. The male form of *G. elliptica* is commonly grown, as it is superior to the female for decoration because its slender grey-green catkins are much longer. This fine evergreen makes a marvellous display throughout this month and next. It can be grown as a free-standing shrub but may be cut by the weather and is usually best grown against a sunny wall where it will be sheltered from cold winds. Grown thus it will reach a height of up to 15 ft (4·5 m). It has no special soil needs, except good drainage.

Hamamelis mollis (Witch Hazel). The best witch hazel is *H. mollis*, the Chinese witch hazel, with curious strap-shaped yellow scented flowers that appear from December to February; the foliage is also colourful in autumn. Plants eventually grow 12 to 15 ft (3·75 to 4·5 m) tall, and as much in width, but this takes some years. A superb variety is *pallida* with large, sulphur-yellow flowers.

Salix (Willow). *S. alba vitellina britzensis* is one of the finest willows for its red shoots, a lovely sight in winter. As the best colour is from the young bark, all are pruned hard each March to encourage plenty of new growth. Like all willows it will do well in ordinary soils as well as the very moist soil it most likes.

FEBRUARY

Cornus mas (Cornelian Cherry). The slow-growing *C. mas*, which bears its small yellow flowers on the bare branch this month, makes a tree of shrub-like habit perhaps 15 to 20 ft (4·5 to 6 m) tall. It has no special soil requirements.

Corylopsis. The most commonly grown species is *C.*

spicata, a deciduous shrub with primrose-yellow flowers that appear before the leaves. The flowers can be spoilt by frost and a sheltered position away from early morning sun is desirable. The plants grow about 6 ft (2 m) tall and as much in width when mature. This is another shrub which likes a moist soil.

Daphne. The species most commonly seen is *D. mezereum*, the mezereon, with fragrant purple or white flowers before the leaves, from February to April. It grows rather narrowly upright to a height of 4 ft (1·25 m) and is excellent for small gardens. It responds to a good soil and this should hold plenty of moisture while still being well·drained.

Elaeagnus. There is no particular reason why *Elaeagnus pungens maculata* should be mentioned now for this shrub with the yellow-splashed leaves is handsome the year round. However, in February, when the weather is usually at its worst, its gaiety is perhaps most welcome of all. It makes a shrub about 5 ft (1·5 m) tall and wide, and has no special soil or other cultural needs.

MARCH

Chaenomeles (Japanese Quince). The Japanese quinces, popularly known as japonica or cydonia, are valuable for their early spring flowers. They can be trained on walls or allowed to grow as bushes in a border in sun or partial shade. Moreover there are numerous varieties and hybrids of *C. speciosa* with pink, white or red flowers. Knap Hill Scarlet, orange-scarlet, makes a bush up to 6 ft (2 m) tall; Rowallane with bright red blooms grows to 4 ft (1·25 m); and Moerloosii, apple-blossom pink, grows to 7 ft (2·25 m).

Forsythia. This is one of the easiest shrubs to grow and with very little attention will produce masses of yellow flowers each year, provided the birds do not pick out its buds in winter. One of the most popular kinds is *F. intermedia spectabilis* which will make a bush 10 ft (3 m) tall with rich deep yellow flowers. The variety Lynwood has even larger flowers.

Another variety of quite recent introduction from the United States is Beatrix Farrand, with large golden-yellow flowers. All grow 10 to 12 ft (3 to 3·75 m) tall.

Then there is *F. suspensa*, an especially good shrub for a north wall, which, at this time of year, bears pale yellow flowers in abundance on its semi-pendulous branches.

Magnolia. One of the most delightful of the magnolias, very early flowering (this month and next) and small growing, is *M. stellata*, the star magnolia. This has the great advantage, too, of coming into flower while still quite young. The common name alludes to the very attractive white flowers. At most this makes a spreading bush 6 to 10 ft (2 to 3 m) tall, and it is slow growing, an advantage in smaller gardens. It is an excellent shrub for town gardens, but like many other magnolias is not happy on limy soils.

APRIL

Berberis (Barberry). The large genus *Berberis* includes some outstanding garden shrubs (including several evergreen kinds for hedging purposes, see p. 76), some valuable for their flowers, others for their foliage and berries. They will do well, moreover, in sun or light shade, but plant small, young specimens whenever possible as this shrub sometimes resists being moved.

Coming into flower this month are those superb evergreen species *B. darwinii* and *B. stenophylla*, both of which have deep yellow flowers. They make large shrubs which are useful as background plants, growing to a height of 8 to 10 ft (2·5 to 3 m) and having a similar spread. *B. stenophylla* has very attractive arching branches.

Camellia. For many years the misconception has been widespread that camellias are tender, although I am sure that more and more gardeners are realizing that this is not so. The many varieties of the evergreen *C. japonica* are perfectly hardy, although their blooms are liable to damage from spring frosts. What they must have is a lime-free, cool, moist soil and they should be planted so that they are shaded from the early morning sun, which is so damaging to the blooms after a frosty night. A west- or north-facing aspect is the best. Where a camellia does get a good deal of sun it will need ample water in the summer and a good mulch to conserve moisture in the soil.

Magnolia stellata **is a useful early-flowering shrub which flowers prolifically during March and April**

It is surprising how early these lovely evergreens come into flower, grown in sheltered conditions. Indeed, the C. *japonica* varieties I have already mentioned and the C. *williamsii* hybrids – which have the merit of dropping, rather than holding on to, their spent blooms – make magnificent wall shrubs.

Fine *japonica* varieties include Lady Clare, soft pink and semi-double; Adolphe Audusson, crimson and semi-double; Elegans, rose-pink and anemone flowered; and Mathotiana Rosea, a rose-pink double. Of the *williamsii* varieties, the magnificent pink, semi-double Donation must be mentioned; also blush-pink single J. C. Williams and Mary Christian, bright pink and single.

Pieris. The most striking kind is *P. formosa forrestii* (especially in its Wakehurst form) which not only has sprays of white flowers rather like lily-of-the-valley, but also young shoots which are bright red. It is an evergreen but must be grown in lime-free soil containing plenty of peat. Plants need a sheltered position and in good conditions will grow 7 ft (2·25 m) tall and as much across.

Ribes (Flowering Currant). The flowering currants, *R. sangineum* and its varieties, are easy-going shrubs that succeed in almost any soil and situation. It is best to plant specially selected forms such as Pulborough Scarlet or King Edward VII, both with deep crimson flowers. Most kinds grow 8 to 10 ft (2·5 to 3 m) tall and spread rapidly, but they can be hard pruned after flowering if it is necessary to keep them smaller.

Spiraea. A spring shrub which has grace and can be reckoned to do well in most conditions is the bridal wreath, *S. arguta*, which bears masses of tiny white flowers just now on arched stems also adorned with attractive little leaves of fresh green. The flowering period spills over into May, which gives it the common name of foam of May – not a bad description.

Ulex. The double form of the common gorse, *U. europaeus plenus,* is an especially useful shrub for dry, sunny banks. It reaches 4 to 5 ft (1·25 to 1·5 m) tall and wide.

MAY

Ceanothus. Blue is something we can never have too much of in the garden and the ceanothus (the Californian lilacs as they are sometimes called) are among the best providers of that colour. A superb ceanothus for growing against a warm, sunny wall in a sheltered position is the low-growing, evergreen *C. thyrsiflorus repens* which literally smothers itself with rich blue flowers during this month. It only grows some 3 ft (1 m) tall too, with a spread of up to 10 ft (3 m), which makes it ideal for

Attractive clusters of white bell-like flowers and bright red young shoots make *Pieris formosa forrestii* a doubly valuable garden shrub. It prefers a sheltered spot and, like rhododendrons, it needs a lime-free soil

growing under a window. Any well-drained soil is suitable.

The deciduous kinds, however, are hardier than the evergreens and some of these are recommended for summer colour (see p. 60).

Cytisus (Broom). There are two cytisuses which deserve special mention for their contribution to the garden in May – *C. kewensis*, a low mat of pale yellow flowers and about 1 ft (30 cm) high by 5 ft (1·5 m) wide, and *C. praecox* which makes a mass of nicely arched branches wreathed this month with cream-coloured flowers. It reaches a height of 4 to 5 ft (1·25 to 1·5 m) and has an equal spread.

Any reasonable soil will suit these shrubs, provided it is well drained, and they must have all the sunshine which is available.

Genista (Broom). These are, of course, relatives of the cytisuses just mentioned and they like the same growing conditions. There isn't a better shrub for a rock garden than *Genista* Lydia which makes a mass of arching stems on which are borne in May and June masses of rich yellow pea flowers. It grows about 2 ft (60 cm) tall and has a spread of up to 5 or 6 ft (1·5 to 2 m).

The other May-flowering genista is *G. hispanica*, the Spanish gorse, which also flowers with abandon in May and June to make a dome of golden-yellow. It can be put to many uses and is especially good for growing on a hot, dry bank.

Kolkwitzia. Nothing like so well known as it deserves to be is *K. amabilis*, the beauty bush, a deciduous shrub which will grow well in any reasonable soil in a sunny position. It makes a bush 6 to 9 ft (2 to 2·75 m) tall and wide and bears in May and June masses of pink, yellow-throated flowers reminiscent of foxgloves.

Rhododendron. In addition to the well-known evergreen kinds, all the azaleas belong in this genus. The deciduous azaleas produce masses of flowers in a wealth of colours. Equally dazzling in their brightest forms, though containing some softer lavenders and pinks as well, are the dwarf evergreen azaleas such as Hinodegiri and Hinomayo. The hardy hybrid rhododendrons, including such well-known kinds as Pink Pearl and Britannia, scarlet, make large bushes with big trusses of flower in shades of red, blue, yellow and white.

An interesting development in recent years has been the introduction of a range of hybrids from the low-growing, white-flowered Japanese species *R. yakushimanum*. These make shapely bushes up to 4 to 5 ft (1·25 to 1·5 m) tall bearing masses of flowers of fine colour and form, many with handsome foliage inherited from this species.

There are others, too, which have the additional attraction of handsome foliage. The leaves of the rather tender *R. williamsianum* (excellent for gardens in the milder areas of Britain) are round and only an inch or two across. Bushes of this form low mounds, not much more than 2 ft (60 cm) in height, with pink flowers.

All rhododendrons must have soil free from lime. They benefit from mulching each spring with moist peat or decayed leaves.

Syringa (Lilac). May and early June is the time of the lilacs, the varieties of *S. vulgaris*, popular not only for their beauty and fragrance but for their ease of cultivation. It pays, however, to dig the soil over well before planting.

Varieties of special worth are the double purple-lavender Katherine Havemeyer; deep red Charles Joly; and Souvenir d'Alice Harding, white; and, among the singles, Maud Notcutt, white; Congo, lilac red; and Massena, purple.

Weigela. Until recently called *Diervilla*, these are easily grown shrubs with masses of pink or red tubular flowers. There are numerous named varieties which include Bristol Ruby, light crimson; Styriaca, deep rose; and Newport Red, deep red. These grow about 6 ft (2 m) tall and a little more in width, but can be kept smaller by pruning after flowering, when the branches that have flowered can be cut out.

Somewhat smaller growing is the decorative *W. florida variegata* which bears very pretty delicate pink flowers this month and in June. The flowers are set off well by the cream-margined foliage.

JUNE

Cistus (Rock Rose). The shrubs are very free-flowering evergreens with blooms like some of the wild roses – hence the common name. They like a hot, sunny situation and well-drained soil. *C. purpureus* grows 4 to 5 ft (1·25 to 1·5 m) tall and about 6 ft (2 m) in width; the rose-pink flowers have a dark zone in the centre. Silver Pink, 3 ft (1 m) tall and 4 ft (1·25 m) across, is a good variety with pale pink flowers and *C. cyprius*, 6 ft (2 m) tall and rather more wide, has large white flowers. All are a little tender and may be killed in very severe winters.

Deutzia. No trouble at all to grow in sunshine or light shade, the deutzias make medium-sized shrubs 5 to 6 ft (1·5 to 2 m) tall and less across. One of the best is Mont Rose with rose-pink blooms; another the very compact *D. rosea* with warm pink blooms. There is also a good white variety named Avalanche. Any ordinary soil will do.

Erica (Heather). Provided you have a lime-free soil and a sunny home to offer them there are some very attractive heathers for flowering between now and September – such as the varieties of *E. cinerea*, the bell heather. These low-growing ericas include the ruby-red *atrorubens*; pink C. G. Best; P. S. Patrick which is purple flowered, and C. D. Eason, pink. Excellent golden-leaved varieties include Golden Drop whose golden-copper foliage turns to a dull red shade in winter.

Escallonia. Outstandingly good seaside shrubs, the evergreen escallonias are a bit on the tender side. Even so, it is often possible to see them growing well in quite unexpected situations. All have fine glossy foliage and make shrubs of medium to large size.

Some of the most reliable in terms of hardiness are the lovely Apple Blossom with pink and white blooms; the crimson C. F. Ball; apple-blossom pink Slieve Donard; and Edinensis, pink.

Hebe. The evergreen shrubs we used to know as veronicas are very useful if rather, for the most part, on the tender side. All are excellent for seaside gardens; they will grow well in all soils, including chalk, and revel in sunshine. Some, like the low-growing, violet-flowered

Helianthemum Brilliant is a brightly coloured rock rose which is seen to best advantage when allowed to tumble over boulders on a rock garden

Carl Teschner, the violet-blue Autumn Glory and the white-flowered *H. pinguifolia pagei*, are excellent for ground-cover purposes. The small foliage is an attraction in itself, that of Carl Teschner being dark green, that of Autumn Glory having a purplish caste and *pagei* having a bluish-grey colouring.

Helianthemum (Sun or Rock roses). These are dwarf evergreen shrubs which put on a wonderful display of colour in early summer. They are sun lovers and ideal for clothing banks, dry walls and, of course, for pockets in the rock garden, thriving on poor soil. The colour range is excellent.

Helianthemum nummularium make very good ground cover and include varieties like the golden-yellow Ben Fhada; The Bride, cream; Ben Nevis, yellow and red; Wisley Primrose, pale yellow; and Ben More, orange.

Jasminum. From late in the month until approximately late August the summer jasmine, *J. officinale*, provides a display with its fragrant white flowers, which are borne in profusion. This climber likes a sunny position and is happy in any kind of garden soil.

Kalmia. A choice evergreen belonging to the same family as the rhododendrons and heathers – *Ericaceae* – is *K. latifolia*, the calico bush, and, consequently, it demands a lime-free soil and light shade. The beautiful pink flowers are quite small and are well set off by the glossy foliage. It makes a shrub 6 ft (2 m) tall and a little less across.

Potentilla (Shrubby Cinquefoil). The varieties of *P. fruticosa* with bright yellow or white buttercup-like flowers are valuable for their long flowering season from June to October. Good varieties are *arbuscula* which makes a wide spreading low bush with yellow flowers; Katherine Dykes, 5 ft (1·5 m) high and through, yellow; Elizabeth, bright primrose yellow, 4 ft (1·25 m); Tangerine, orange-yellow, 2 ft (60 cm), and Mount Everest, 3 ft high and through, white.

Viburnum. A large shrub, 8 to 10 ft (2·5 to 3 m) tall and wide – for flowering this month, sometimes a little earlier – is *V. opulus sterile*, the snowball tree, which gets its name from the large creamy-white, ball-like blooms. There is also good autumn colour from the leaves.

JULY

Buddleia. There are few shrubs that give such a good show for so little attention as the sun-loving varieties of *B. davidii*. The flowers can be had in various shades of purple and lilac as well as white, and if the old stems are pruned hard in early March fine flower spikes are produced in the summer. Plants can be kept to a height of about 6 ft (2 m) by such annual pruning, and will have a similar spread. Good varieties include the deep purple Black Knight; the reddish-purple Royal Red; and White Cloud.

Another beautiful species with lavender flowers all along the stems is *B. alternifolia*. As the stems are pendulous it is best grown as a standard on a long main stem when it forms an attractive small tree.

Hypericum (St John's Wort). These very accommodating deciduous shrubs grow well in any ordinary soil which is well drained. The best of them is *Hypericum* Hidcote which bears a mass of saucer-shaped golden blooms from now until the autumn.

Perovskia (Russian Sage). A useful semi-woody shrub for late summer but only for sunny positions, *P. atriplici-*

Easily grown in almost any situation, *Hypericum patulum* Hidcote is a colourful choice for an empty corner in the garden. It is planted here between *Philadelphus coronarius* and a golden-foliaged privet

folia, up to 7 ft (2·25 m) tall, has lavender-blue flowers and grey, sage-like foliage. The variety Blue Spire is an improvement on the type.

Senecio. *Senecio laxifolius* is a valuable shrub both for its grey evergreen foliage and its masses of yellow, daisy-like flowers in summer. It has a rather spreading habit and succeeds well in poor, well-drained soil in a sunny position. It is also good near the sea. Plants do not grow much more than 3 to 4 ft (1 to 1·25 m) in height but may be twice that in width.

AUGUST

Ceanothus. There are both evergreen and deciduous kinds but the latter tend to be hardier and more reliable, as I have already remarked, and they flower in late summer when the number of shrubs in bloom is far more restricted than in May–June, the season of the evergreen ceanothus. Gloire de Versailles, pale blue, and Henri Desfosse, deep violet, are good deciduous varieties. Their height and spread is 5 to 6 ft (1·5 to 2 m), if cut hard back each April.

Erica (Heather). The varieties of the Cornish heath, *E. vagans,* around 1½ ft (45 cm) tall go on flowering from now until October which is very valuable – but, of course, they must have lime-free soil. I would especially recommend Mrs D. F. Maxwell, a lovely deep cerise colour; Lyonesse, which is white with contrasting brown anthers; and St Keverne, which is rose-pink in colour.

Hibiscus. These are valuable for their hollyhock-like flowers in late summer but they need a position in full sun. There are numerous varieties of *H. syriacus,* such as Coeleste, blue; Woodbridge, red; and Blue Bird, a fine blue. They will reach a height of about 8 ft (2·5 m) and nearly as much through but are slow growing.

Hydrangea. In addition to the familiar mop-headed Hortensia hydrangeas, there are the less well-known Lacecaps with large coloured bracts surrounding a flattish disc of tiny flowers. There are numerous varieties of both types but the colour does depend on the soil. In lime-free soils the flowers tend towards blue and purple whereas on limy soils they tend towards pink and red. Alum applied to the soil can be used to change the flowers from red to blue but this is difficult if there is a lot of lime present. White varieties remain white whatever the soil. Two fine Lacecaps are Bluewave, blue or lilac, and Whitewave, white. Good mop-heads are Generale Vicomtesse de Vibraye, blue or pink; Westfalen, crimson or violet; Hamburg, deep pink or blue; and Madame E. Mouillière, white. The flower buds for the following year are formed at the tips of the shoots made in the previous year. In cold districts, where frost

A planting of herbaceous perennials and dwarf or slow-growing shrubs, where year-round colour is ensured by the presence of subjects with overlapping flowering periods. Dwarf conifers provide foliage effects

The brilliant crimson, scarlet and orange tints of *Acer palmatum*, the Japanese maple, make it an important source of autumn colour. A number of different varieties are available, many with attractively cut foliage

can damage the buds, flowering is not likely to be good unless protection is given.

There are one or two others which must not be overlooked. Preziosa makes a bush about 4 ft (1·25 m) tall and through and is very attractive with the stems and young leaves both having a purplish tinge, while the Hortensia-type round flowers start off a rose-pink and deepen in colour with age. *H. paniculata grandiflora* is bigger (up to 10 ft [3 m] tall and wide) and bears very large panicles of flowers this month and next which start off white and fade to pink. This makes a fine specimen shrub for a lawn.

Pernettya. An excellent small-growing (3 ft [1 m] tall) evergreen shrub for lime-free peaty soils in sun or light shade is *P. mucronata* and its varieties which, from now onwards, bear berries that persist through the winter. These are coloured in shades from purple to red, pink, lavender and white, but to get berries both male and female forms must be grown. They are excellent when planted with rhododendrons and azaleas.

SEPTEMBER

Caryopteris. Particularly valuable for its late blue flowers and greyish foliage, *C. clandonensis* can grow 3 to 4 ft (1 to 1·25 m) tall and almost as much across, although plants can be kept shorter by pruning back the shoots each April. Two modern varieties with good dark blue flowers are Ferndown and Kew Blue.

Fuchsia. There are many varieties, with flowers as attractive as the greenhouse kinds, that can be grown in the open if the base of the plant is mounded with sand, peat or weathered ashes as protection in the winter. The stems may be cut back to ground level by frost but new growth should shoot from the base in the spring and flower in late summer. The fuchsia that is often seen near the sea is *F. magellanica riccartonii* which has small red and purple flowers. *F. m. versicolor* not only has carmine and purple flowers but also attractive foliage variegated with silver and·pink. Lena, pale pink and mauve; Margaret, carmine and parma violet; Corallina, scarlet and purple; and Mrs Popple, crimson and violet, are other varieties well worth growing.

OCTOBER

Acer (Maple). Most of the maples are trees, but the varieties of *A. palmatum* are shrubby and valuable for their handsome foliage which colours magnificently in autumn. The leaves of the variety *purpureum* are deep purple throughout the summer and those of *dissectum atropurpureum* are not only purple throughout but also finely cut, like those of a fern. Both grow slowly and take years to reach a height of 6 to 8 ft (2 to 2·5 m).

Cotoneaster. The many kinds, both deciduous and evergreen, are of particular value for their berries, although the flowers are not uninteresting. *C. horizontalis* sends out its shoots horizontally, is deciduous and has masses of red berries. It looks particularly well against a wall or covering a rock. *C. conspicuus decorus* is an evergreen bush of rounded habit, 3 to 4 ft (1 to 1·25 m) high with scarlet berries. *C. franchetii* is a more open shrub with arching branches to 8 ft (2·5 m) and as much through, also with scarlet berries. *C. salicifolius* Autumn Fire (Herbstfeuer), growing only 1 ft (30 cm) tall, carpets ground quickly and is excellent on banks. This bears orange-red berries freely in autumn. Another spreader with berries of similar colouring is Skogholm – also excellent for ground cover.

Fothergilla. The hazel-like leaves turn a lovely shade of yellow in the autumn and in April–May produce creamy-white flower spikes. *F. monticola* is one of the best kinds growing to a height and breadth of about 5 ft (1·5 m). No fothergilla grows well on lime or chalk soils.

NOVEMBER

Berberis (Barberry). It is the deciduous kinds that produce abundant crops of scarlet or coral berries in the autumn. *B. wilsoniae*, which makes a dense, spiny bush 4 to 5 ft (1·25 to 1·5 m) high, is a fine example of this type and so are *B. aggregata* and *B.* Cherry Ripe.

Erica. An especially useful attribute of the many varieties of the winter-flowering heather, *E. carnea*, is their lime tolerance which gives them much adaptability. Indeed, they can be used to give the garden colour right through from this month to spring, together with the *darleyensis* hybrids.

But to take the *carnea* varieties first, Eileen Porter, carmine red, is in flower by now, followed by the pink-flowered King George next month, and from the New Year onwards such good things as Springwood Pink and Springwood White; Pink Spangles, the carmine Vivellii and the dark red Ruby Glow take one through to the spring. Aurea and Foxhollow provide golden foliage which also enlivens the colours with which they are associated.

Among the *darleyensis* hybrids the pink, late-winter flowering Jack H. Brummage also provides golden foliage; Arthur Johnson bears magenta blooms right through from November to spring; and Silberschmelze is a fine white also with a very long flowering season.

Pyracantha (Firethorn). The firethorns are showy evergreen shrubs with masses of red or yellow berries in autumn and winter and abundant white flowers in May and June. They can be trained to walls – they do well on those with north aspects – or grown as bushes in the open. Most grow 10 ft (3 m) tall and as wide. *P. coccinea lalandei* with bright red berries is the type most commonly seen but the yellow-berried *P. rogersiana flava* is very well worth growing. Another excellent variety is Orange Glow.

Skimmia. An evergreen growing 3 to 4 ft (1 to 1·25 m) tall, with large bright red berries. The type to grow is *S. foremanii* as it has both male and female flowers on the same bush and bears regular crops of berries in the winter. It will grow well in shade.

DECEMBER

Jasminum (Jasmine). The hardy *J. nudiflorum*, winter jasmine is a fine climber for winter colour. It has yellow flowers and will grow even on walls with a north aspect. The strong, rather angular growth will eventually reach a height of 15 ft (4·5 m).

Viburnum. There are both deciduous and evergreen kinds, not all winter flowering. *V. tinus*, generally known as laurustinus, starts to open its clusters of white flowers – pink in the bud stage – in late autumn and continues well into the spring. *V. fragrans* is deciduous with pretty pink and white scented flowers which appear from November to February. *V. bodnantense* has larger deeper pink flowers but a stiffer, slightly ungainly habit. Dawn is the variety of *bodnantense* usually grown but there is another, Deben, which remains even longer in flower. All grow to a height of 10 ft (3 m).

Trees for Colour

The typical modern, fairly small garden may not give wide scope for the use of ornamental trees, but those that can be included in the scheme of things have an importance out of all proportion to their numbers. One should not forget when planning or re-modelling a garden the transformation in scale which can be brought about by planting only one or two trees in carefully chosen positions. Naturally one must choose trees of suitable dimensions, and consider which are likely to make the most valuable contribution to the general scheme of things – whether they have flowers of fine form and colouring, handsome leaves or bark, or just an elegance of habit which will give added point to other adjacent garden features.

Colour for All Seasons

Acer (Maple). Many of the maples make large trees, too tall for small gardens, and the Japanese maples (varieties of *A. palmatum*) have been described in the previous chapter on shrubs, but intermediate between these there are species and varieties supremely well suited to the smaller garden. One of particular merit is the paperbark maple, *A. griseum*, which grows to a height of 40 ft (12 m) or so. The common name comes from the bark which peels thinly to show the orange-red trunk underneath. The shapely leaves colour beautifully in autumn. Also good for autumn colour is *A. grosseri hersii* which has attractive white-lined bark and makes a tree up to 30 ft (9 m) in height. *A. negundo variegatum*, 25 ft (7.5 m) or so, is one of the best small trees for town gardens. The leaves are attractively variegated with white.

Amelanchier lamarckii. This small tree pays a double dividend in the shape of a profusion of small white flowers which clothe the bare branches in April and leaves which turn brilliant red before they fall in autumn.

It grows up to 25 ft (7.5 m) tall and as much across.

Arbor-vitae, see Thuja

Arbutus unedo (Strawberry Tree). The evergreen strawberry tree is an attractive choice where colour and interest late in the year is desired. It should be planted in a sheltered position because of its late flowering. The panicles of white flowers are borne at the same time as the strawberry-like fruits in late autumn and are very decorative. The leaves are a splendid foil for these, being dark green and glossy. Unlike most ericaceous plants, *A. unedo* grows well in limy soils. It may reach 25 ft (7.5 m) or rather more in height but is more likely to be nearer 15 ft (4.5 m) tall. It is especially useful for planting in coastal districts.

Betula (Birch). Although so common, and an offender in so much as it is a notorious soil robber, the birch in its numerous forms is a beautiful tree for many different settings. The colour of the bark and the lovely tracery of the bare branches in winter make this very much a tree of year-round interest. A popular variety is Young's weeping birch, *B. pendula youngii*, which makes a splendid lawn specimen. Another variety of *B. pendula* which has value for confined spaces is *fastigiata*, of erect habit rather like a Lombardy poplar. Both these grow to 30 ft (9 m) or so in height.

A particularly graceful variety of *B. pendula* is the Swedish birch, *B. p. dalecarlica*, which although it grows to a height of 40 ft (12 m) or more is not very broad and therefore is suitable for planting in many gardens. The branches arch over and the leaves are deeply and very prettily cut giving the tree much appeal. Two birches with very white trunks should also be included – *B. ermanii* and the paper birch, *B. papyrifera*, with thinly peeling bark. Both make trees of large size (up to 50 to 60 ft, 15 to 18 m) and need spacious surroundings to do them justice.

Cedrus (Cedar). It needs a large garden to consider planting any of the cedars. The beautiful cedar of Lebanon, *C. libani*, needs no introduction, and mention must be made of *C. atlantica glauca*, an attractive variety of the Atlas cedar with beautiful glaucous blue foliage and arching branches. Remember, though, that this tree can reach a height of around 100 ft (30 m) and have a spread of perhaps 50 ft (15 m). An open, sunny situation is desirable.

Chamaecyparis. This is an important genus for the intending planter, although most of them make large trees. The dwarf varieties do not concern us here. *C. lawsoniana*, the Lawson's cypress, can reach a height of 100 ft (30 m) but many of its excellent varieties are of more modest stature. A few of special interest for their colouring are the pyramidal, glaucous green *allumii*, about 40 ft (12 m) tall; *lutea*, golden foliaged, also about 40 ft (12 m) tall and called the golden Lawson's cypress; and Triomphe de Boskoop, about 50 ft (15 m) tall with handsome glaucous blue foliage and a pyramidal habit.

Cherry, see Prunus

Crab Apple, see Malus

Crataegus (Thorn). There are various ornamental thorns which make good garden trees for open sunny positions, and one of the best is *C. oxyacantha coccinea plena*, Paul's double scarlet thorn, which is a picture in May when carrying its mantle of rosy-red flowers. This, too, is a tree of about 20 ft (6 m) in height.

Cupressocyparis leylandii. Extremely fast growing and with a columnar habit, this cross between *Cupressus macrocarpa* and *Chamaecyparis nootkatensis* is a fine specimen tree. It is a very good seaside conifer and does well on chalk. The foliage is dark green. It may reach a height of 60 ft (18 m). It is a first-rate hedging conifer and has an exceptionally fast rate of growth – often as much as 2 to 3 ft (60 cm to 1 m) in a year. There is now a decorative golden-yellow variety, Castlewellan, which can also be used for the same purpose. They will tolerate a wide range of conditions.

Davidia (Handkerchief Tree). For those gardeners who can provide a sheltered home for it where the soil is reasonably moist there is no more distinctive tree to grow than *D. involucrata vilmoriniana*, the so-called handkerchief tree or dove tree introduced from China at the end of the last century. In May a good specimen is an unforgettable sight bearing a mass of huge white bracts around rather insignificant green flowers, two bracts to each flower, just occasionally three. These bracts are made the more attractive by the fresh green colouring of the heart-shaped leaves. Usually the handkerchief tree will grow to 30 ft (9 m) or so tall but it can reach 50 ft (15 m) or more. The bracts are not usually produced on specimens below 15 years of age.

Dawn Redwood, see Metasequoia

Betula pendula youngii, a silver birch with weeping branches, is an ideal tree for a small garden

Eucalyptus (Gum Tree). *E. gunnii* is probably the hardiest of the eucalypts with *E. niphophila* (see below), and it is certainly worth growing, in well-drained soil in warmer gardens, for its distinctive foliage. When mature – and it is a fast grower – it can make a tree 50 ft (15 m) tall. Juvenile specimens have glaucous blue and rounded leaves and adult trees, grey-green, long and narrow, pointed leaves. To keep the characteristic rounded foliage of the juvenile form, *E. gunnii* should be pruned each year in March.

Another eucalypt which is coming to the fore, however, is the handsome snow gum, *E. niphophila*. This is proving as hardy as any gum coming, as it does, from heights of up to 6,500 ft (1,950 m) in the mountainous regions of New South Wales and Victoria in its native Australia. It is still a relative newcomer here but will probably make a tree of about 30 ft (9 m) or more.

False Acacia, see Robinia

Golden Rain Tree, see Laburnum

Gum Tree, see Eucalyptus

Halesia monticola (Snowdrop Tree). This can be grown as a shrub or small tree in lime-free soils. It is very beautiful indeed when carrying its bell-shaped white flowers in May.

Handkerchief Tree, see Davidia

Variegated hollies provide year-round interest. If a female variety is purchased, berries are a bonus

Ilex (Holly). The hollies usually grown are varieties of *I. aquifolium*, the common holly, and these include many with attractive variegated leaves. These are very accommodating plants which will grow well in the open or semi-shade. An excellent variety with silver variegation is the female *argenteo-marginata*. (It should be noted that both male and female varieties should be planted if good crops of berries are required.) For gold variegation an excellent variety is Madame Briot. Both these varieties will reach a height of around 20 ft (6 m).

Consider also the excellent golden-variegated and free-berrying *I. altaclarensis* Golden King (female, despite its name) which grows to a height of about 25 ft (7·5 m).

Juniperus (Juniper). A juniper which has considerable value from our point of view is the Irish juniper, *J. communis hibernica*. This has a columnar habit and glaucous foliage and will eventually – for it is slow growing – reach a height of 10 to 15 ft (3 to 4·5 m). It likes lime in the soil.

Koelreuteria paniculata. This is an attractive, easily pleased tree which bears yellow flowers in summer and follows these with a display of bladder-like fruits. The foliage turns rich yellow in autumn. Although it can grow to 40 ft (12 m) tall, *K. paniculata* is more likely to be around 25 ft (7·5 m).

Laburnum (Golden Rain Tree). The laburnums in their various forms are splendid trees for gardens of all sizes but one must be aware that the seeds are poisonous and can therefore be a hazard if there are young children in the family. Best of all is *L. vossii*, with long racemes of rich yellow flowers, which makes a tree of 15 to 25 ft (4·5 to 7·5 m) tall and is a cross between the common laburnum, *L. anagyroides*, and the Scotch laburnum, *L. alpinum*.

Lawson's Cypress, see Chamaecyparis

Liquidambar (Sweet Gum). If you have the space, an open position and moist, loamy soil, there is no finer tree for rich crimson autumn colour than *L. styraciflua*; but with a height of 60 ft (18 m) and a spread almost as great it is not many gardeners who can indulge the luxury of growing this tree.

Magnolia. I shall mention only a few of the many lovely magnolias available, namely the popular 30-ft (9-m) tall *M. soulangiana*, which, with its numerous forms, is a superb town tree, among other things; *M. denudata*, a lovely species of about 25 ft (7·5 m) with white, cup-shaped flowers; and the evergreen *M. grandiflora* which grows well as a wall plant and bears fragrant, cup-shaped, creamy-white flowers from July to September. *M. soulangiana*, with large white flowers suffused with purple on the outside, provides a display in April and May and *M. denudata* comes into flower in early March. The latter may have its flowers damaged by frost.

All of the magnolias like a rich, well-drained soil, preferably free of lime.

Malus (Flowering and Fruiting Crabs). The flowering crabs make excellent trees for gardens of all sizes, many of them being in the 15 to 20 ft (4·5 to 6 m) height range although others reach 40 ft (12 m) or so. Of special interest are the deep crimson-flowered *M. lemoinei*, the pink-flowered *M. floribunda* (both about 25 ft· [7·5 m] tall) and the fine fruiting crabs, Golden Hornet (yellow fruits), John Downie (yellow and red fruits) and Dartmouth (reddish-purple fruits). The crabs will grow well in any reasonable soil and in open positions.

Maple, see Acer

Metasequoia glyptostroboides (Dawn Redwood). This very handsome fossil-age deciduous conifer, re-discovered in China in 1945, is certainly worth a place in many gardens. Its graceful habit and feathery foliage make it very attractive and the leaves turn a glorious shade of pinkish-brown in autumn. It has still not been in cultivation long enough to know its ultimate height, but already there are trees over 50 ft (15 m) in height and a specimen in its native country has been recorded as being 115 ft (34·5 m) tall. So 70 ft (21 m) or more must be allowed for.

Mountain Ash, see Sorbus

Picea (Spruce). Many of the spruces are too large for garden planting but the slow-growing *P. pungens glauca*, the Blue Spruce, makes a handsome small tree with rich blue-grey glaucous foliage. Give this tree a sunny position.

Prunus. This genus includes the flowering cherries, plums, peaches, apricots and almonds, and other trees like the cherry laurel and Portugal laurel. The value of the spring-flowering cherries, almonds and peaches is

The flowers of *Malus floribunda*, which is sometimes known as the Japanese crab, are carried in profusion on arching branches in May. The deep pink of the unopened buds form a pleasant combination with the paler shell pink of the open flowers. This plant will eventually form an umbrella-shaped tree some 25 ft (7·5 m) in height but it is particularly handsome in its youth when its branches are held at eye level. The bold foliage of *Bergenia cordifolia* contrasts well with the delicacy of the tree

very great indeed, as their popularity bears witness. The flowering cherries will grow well in almost any reasonable garden soil but the almonds and peaches are better in a warm, sheltered position in a well-drained soil of rather better quality.

Cherries of especial value, in my opinion, are the pure white, single-flowered Shirotae; the fastigiate, semi-double, pink Amanogawa (so useful with its narrow, upright habit for confined spaces), and the even more

Robinia pseudoacacia Frisia is a breathtaking sight from late spring to autumn when the vivid yellow leaves become slightly coppery. Each leaf is composed of many oval leaflets which give the tree a feathery appearance

useful columnar *P. hillieri* Spire which besides putting on a display of pink flowers in spring also provides excellent autumn leaf colour; the double, white Shirofugen; the double, rosy-pink Kanzan; and Pink Perfection, with double, carmine-pink flowers. Kanzan is taller than the others by at least 10 ft (3 m), growing up to 40 ft (12 m) in height. A lovely peach is *P. persica* Clara Meyer which only grows to about 15 ft (4.5 m) tall; an almond of merit is the double *P. communis roseo-plena*, with pale pink flowers. (See the remarks on colour combinations on p. 19.)

For autumn and winter flowering there is *P. subhirtella autumnalis*, which produces its semi-double white or pale pink flowers intermittently throughout the months from November to March. The purple-leaved plum, *P. cerasifera pissardii*, with pink flowers, is very useful indeed for providing foliage contrasts in mixed planting schemes.

Robinia (False Acacia). The robinias, both trees and shrubs, are excellent plants for growing in towns, given any reasonable soil and a sunny position. The false acacia, *R. pseudoacacia*, makes a tree 70 ft (21 m) or so in height and it has distinctive and very attractive pinnate leaves and white flowers which are borne in early summer. The variety which has become so very popular in recent years, though, is the Dutch-raised Frisia, its attraction being the golden-yellow foliage which retains its good colouring throughout the season until leaf fall.

Robinias, however, have rather a bad name for branch snapping and it is wise to give Frisia, or any other for that matter, a position sheltered from strong winds.

Salix (Willow). The golden weeping willow, *S. alba tristis* (syn. *S. a. vitellina pendula*), is a splendid garden tree where a suitable site can be provided. The attractions, apart from its habit, are the golden stems and bright green leaves. Its especial value for most gardens is that it is of smaller size than the weeping willow proper, *S. babylonica*, which is up to 50 ft (15 m) tall.

Snowdrop Tree, see Halesia

Sorbus (Mountain Ash and Whitebeam). The Mountain Ash, *S. aucuparia*, and its varieties, are suitable trees for town or country gardens, with attractive flowers, fruits and fern-like foliage. An especially good variety for autumn display is *edulis*, which has larger fruits than the others. A noteworthy whitebeam is *S. aria lutescens* which is easily distinguished by the greyish coloured hairs which cover the leaves and give the tree such a handsome appearance.

Spruce, see Picea

Strawberry Tree, see Arbutus

Sweet Gum, see Liquidambar

Taxus (Yew). The English Yew, *T. baccata*, is another tree which needs no introduction, and even bearing in mind its slow rate of growth it is still very valuable for garden planting, where space is available. Where space is limited the Irish yew, *T. b. fastigiata* – which is also available in a golden-leaved form, *aurea* – is an excellent proposition with its upright habit and height of about 15 ft (4.5 m) or so.

Thorn, see Crataegus

Thuja (Arbor-vitae). The variegated form of the Western arbor-vitae, *T. plicata zebrina*, with its foliage banded in green and yellow, is an especially showy member of this genus of conifers. Height up to 30 ft (9 m).

Whitebeam, see Sorbus

Willow, see Salix

Yew, see Taxus

Climbing and Wall Plants for Colour

Walls and fences can easily be made attractive by clothing their nakedness with suitable climbing plants whose flowers or leaves will, in their season, provide much colour and interest – and widen your gardening horizons. Numerous shrubs which are not climbing plants at all are excellent for growing against walls. A sheltered wall may provide just the warm corner for a favourite plant that would not survive in an exposed place in the garden, yet how often we see gardens where the best use is not made of such opportunities. The period of interest can also be extended by planting several different climbers in close proximity to each other.

One must naturally try and match the colour of brick walls with the colours of the plants to be grown. This factor can be overlooked quite easily – as I know well. The neutral colour of stone means that it mixes well with almost anything.

Wherever climbers and wall shrubs are planted they will become permanent features and once planted they should not be disturbed. This means that we must be sure that we choose the right position in the first place and that the soil is thoroughly prepared before planting. There is little that can be done in this respect after planting other than to give a topdressing of compost, peat or old manure in the autumn or early spring, depending on the plants' requirements.

I mention choosing the right place for I have seen camellias, which are not climbers, of course, but are most decorative wall plants, planted in full sun against a south-facing wall because it was imagined that they were tender. The result was that they started to shrivel, but fortunately they were transplanted before it was too late.

Some Recommendations

Abutilon. In milder areas, the dainty *A. megapotamicum* is well worth trying in a south- or west-facing corner, for although it is not a true climber it can be trained against a wall. It grows about 6 ft (2 m) tall and bears a succession of pendant red and yellow lantern-shaped flowers with prominent brownish anthers from June to October. This shrub is a native of Brazil and should be protected in severe weather with sacking or polythene, with a space for air to circulate freely. Gardeners in milder parts of Britain may smile at this suggestion, but many of us have more rigorous conditions to contend with in winter, and, even worse, in late spring.

Actinidia. A striking climber is *A. kolomikta* which has heart-shaped green leaves variegated with pink and white. It is ideal for a position in full sun on a south- or west-facing wall. The colourful leaf variegation is not always present in young specimens but there is the added attraction of small white flowers in June. It can reach a height of 20 ft (6 m) and requires good support and a fertile soil.

Bachelor's Buttons, see Kerria

Bilderdyckia, see Polygonum

Camellia. See p. 53 for description and varieties.

Campsis radicans (Trumpet Creeper). The trumpet creeper, a native of North America and formerly known as *Tecoma* and *Bignonia,* is a handsome, vigorous climber for a warm wall in full sun. As a young plant it may need protection during severe weather, but once established it is reasonably hardy. The large trumpet-shaped scarlet and orange flowers are freely produced in August and September. It climbs to a height of 20 ft (6 m) or more by means of its aerial roots. The Oriental species, *C. grandiflora* (syn. *C. chinensis*), has orange and red blooms but it is not so self-supporting as *C. radicans.*

The pink leaf variegation of *Actinidia kolomikta* is only reliably produced if the plant is grown against a sunny wall. Small white flowers are produced in June

Ceanothus. This is a good way of growing the rather more tender evergreen kinds, see p. 55.

Chaenomeles (Japanese Quince). See description on p. 53.

Chimonanthus praecox (Winter Sweet). A most lovely shrub for growing against a warm south- or west-facing wall is *C. praecox* (syn. *C. fragrans*). This bears pale yellow flowers with purple centres on the bare branches in December and January. The petals have a distinctive waxy appearance. The fragrance is such that just a small flowering shoot left in a room overnight will fill the air with its sweetness. There is a beautiful clear primrose-yellow variety, *luteus*, which comes into flower in February. Both will eventually make shrubs up to 10 ft (3 m) tall and across, if well suited. They like best a rather light soil which is retentive of moisture.

Clematis. These glorious climbing plants are justly popular and there are a great many species and hybrids available from specialist growers – far more different varieties, I am sure, than is generally appreciated. They are grown in pots by nurserymen and are best planted in October and November or in spring. The soil should be moist but at the same time well drained and the lower parts of the plants' stems should be shaded from direct sun.

Clematis are hardy and it is a mistake to plant them

Ceanothus thyrsiflorus is a favourite shrub for planting against a warm wall. Its misty blue flowers are produced in May and June and last for many weeks

against hot walls unless the roots and lower parts of the plants are reasonably cool and moist. Which to plant is a matter of personal preference, but where a quick grower is required to cover an old shed or tree then I suggest *C. montana* which is a mass of star-like white flowers in May and June. There are also one or two pink forms of this species, *rubens* being one which also has attractive bronze-purple leaves in the spring. Another of my favourite clematis is the species *C. macropetala* which bears its beautiful semi-double, blue, pendant flowers at the beginning of summer.

Best of all is the violet-purple hybrid *C. jackmanii* which flowers freely from July to September or even later. Other lovely large-flowered hybrids include the clear pink Comtesse de Bouchaud; the robustly growing, carmine-red Ville de Lyon; the pinkish-mauve Marcel Moser, which has petals marked with a carmine bar; and Lasurstern, purplish-blue with prominent gold stamens, which makes a grand show in May and June and again in September. Another charming variety that flowers in the spring and the autumn is the large, pale mauve-pink Nelly Moser which has a deep carmine bar on each of its petals.

Then there is the evergreen *C. armandii* which starts to flower in late March and bears its white blooms in clusters. The leaves of this species are leathery, pointed and quite different from those of the deciduous varieties. It does best on a sheltered wall as long as the roots are kept moist.

One of the fastest-growing clematis available is *Clematis montana rubens* which will scramble over a wall or building or through the branches of a tall tree

For later in the season there are those two species with yellow flowers and decorative seed heads – C. orientalis and C. tangutica. The first, *orientalis*, has thick-sepalled flowers of bell-shaped appearance. These, which have earned it the common name of orange peel clematis, are borne from August to October and are followed by very attractive silky seed heads. The second, *tangutica*, has delightful deep yellow flowers like Chinese lanterns and these also first appear in August to continue into October, when the last can be enjoyed in company with the silky seed heads. At most these will climb to a height of around 15 ft (4·5 m) and both have attractively divided leaves.

Cotoneaster. The deciduous C. horizontalis with its flat, herringbone-like habit is a splendid wall shrub, decorative for many months of the year but especially so when carrying its crop of red berries in autumn. Reaching a height of 2 to 3 ft (60 cm to 1 m) and having a spread of 8 to 10 ft (2·5 to 3 m) it is well suited for a position under a window or against a low wall which it is desired to screen. The low-growing C. microphyllus, an evergreen with crimson berries, is also useful for growing over retaining walls.

Escallonia macrantha. This evergreen species makes a satisfactory wall shrub. Its habit is rounded and it reaches a height of about 10 ft (3 m). Its light crimson flowers are borne from June to September.

Euonymus. Often used as ground cover, the evergreen E. fortunei radicans will support itself by aerial roots if planted against a wall, either in sun or shade. The variety Silver Queen is more decorative than the species and its broad leaves have a pleasing silver variegation around the margin. This shrub reaches a height of around 10 ft (3 m).

Firethorn, see Pyracantha

Forsythia suspensa. The distinctive F. suspensa with pendulous habit and bright yellow flowers is a good choice for a north or east wall where a shrub of about 10 to 12 ft (3 to 3·75 m) is needed. It flowers in March–early April.

Garrya elliptica. Already described on p. 52, G. elliptica in its male form is another good plant for a sunny, sheltered wall.

Hedera (Ivy). It is the current enthusiasm for house plants which has brought the ornamental ivies to the forefront and very attractive these can be in carefully chosen positions. Two outstanding varieties are H. canariensis variegata, a handsome form of the Canary Island ivy with large, rounded, dark green leaves bordered with silver-white, and H. colchica dentata variegata whose large soft green leaves are broadly margined with pale gold. Both grow to a height of 10 ft (3 m) or so. Many other varieties with leaves of different shapes and sizes are available and will be found listed in good shrub catalogues. All have the merit of growing well with any aspect.

An especially decorative variety of the common ivy, Hedera helix, is Buttercup, with golden young foliage which takes on green hues with age. This grows almost 6 to 7 ft (2 to 2·25 m) tall.

Honeysuckle, see Lonicera

Hydrangea petiolaris. The self-clinging climbing hydrangea H. petiolaris is recommended for a north- or east-facing wall or for growing on a tree to a height of 20 ft (6 m) or more. This deciduous species bears large, flat heads of white flowers in June and July. Not so reliably hardy as H. petiolaris is the deciduous H. anomala, with leaves pleasingly curled and glossy when young. This also is self-clinging and it bears creamy-white flat flowers in June and July.

Itea ilicifolia. If the kerria referred to later is one of the most ubiquitous of shrubs, the evergreen I. ilicifolia is the opposite. This handsome shrub bears long pendulous racemes of catkin-like greenish-white, fragrant flowers in late summer. It should be planted against a south- or west-facing wall and does best in a loamy soil or sandy peat with plenty of moisture. Once established it makes quite quick growth, attaining a height of about 8 ft (2·5 m).

Ivy, see Hedera

The common honeysuckle, *Lonicera periclymenum*, is much valued for the delicious fragrance of its yellow and pink flowers which appear from June onwards

Jasminum (Jasmine). For descriptions of those two excellent climbers, *J. officinale* and *J. nudiflorum*, see pp. 58 and 63 respectively.

Kerria. The fact that bachelor's buttons, *K. japonica pleniflora*, is one of the most frequently seen garden shrubs should not make one pass it over when drawing up planting schemes. It is a pretty shrub in April and May with its mass of ball-like orange-yellow flowers borne on thin, arching stems, and its popularity is a measure of its good-natured acceptance of widely differing conditions. In fact, this deciduous shrub grows well given any aspect and is as happy against a wall or fence as when it is grown as a free-standing specimen. It usually reaches a height of about 10 ft (2·5 m).

Lonicera (Honeysuckle). Among the most lovely, informal climbers are the honeysuckles. Two deliciously fragrant deciduous varieties are the early Dutch (*L. periclymenum belgica*), which flowers in June and July, and the late Dutch (*L. p. serotina*), which follows in August and September. Both have reddish-purple flowers, yellow within. They may be planted with any aspect, but a south-facing wall might prove too hot, at any rate in the south of England.

The evergreen *L. japonica halliana* will also succeed given any aspect and in sun or shade. It is quick growing and bears fragrant flowers – soft creamy-yellow, fading to ochre – from June to October. The individual flowers are small but are neatly arranged in pairs along the whole length of the current year's growth, which accounts for the continuity of flower. It can become untidy, but if the twiggy shoots are cut out in March this will keep it in reasonable order. This is an admirable plant to grow on a trellis or porch.

The large-flowered, deciduous *L. tellmanniana* makes a great show in June and July and does best on a semi-shaded, west-facing wall. Unfortunately, its rich yellow flowers flushed with red are not scented – but in the garden as elsewhere one cannot always have everything. Another evergreen honeysuckle for planting with any aspect is *L. japonica aureo-reticulata* which has oval leaves veined golden-yellow. This is a good climber to plant near the front door of the house where all-season interest is a particular asset.

Parthenocissus. The well-known Virginia creeper *P. quinquefolia* (syn. *Vitis quinquefolia*) is seen at its best when growing up a tall tree with its long trailing growths of fresh green, three- or five-lobed leaves swaying in the breeze. In autumn the leaves turn a spectacular scarlet and orange. It is self-clinging on a wall but it does require ample space or it may grow into guttering and become too exuberant around windows. Outstanding for autumn colour and also a strong grower is *P. tricuspidata* (syn. *Vitis inconstans*) and *P. henryana* (syn. *Vitis henryana*) which will soon cover a large wall. The leaves are variegated pink and white and the characteristic is more pronounced when the plant is growing in partial shade, although it is quite happy in full sun. In autumn the leaves turn brilliant red.

Passiflora caerulea (Passion Flower). In the milder areas of the country where a sheltered, sunny wall can be offered, a showy climber is the Passion flower, *P. caerulea*. It will do well in any reasonable soil, provided it is well drained. The fragrant flowers, up to 4 in (10 cm) across, are distinctive in appearance and a lovely amalgam of white and blue shades. There is also an ivory-white variety, Constance Elliott. The flowers are borne from June to September.

Polygonum baldschuanicum (Russian Vine). The very rampant Russian vine, *P. baldschuanicum* (more correctly *Bilderdyckia baldschuanicum*), might be described as a plant in a hurry. Certainly it is unsurpassed for providing cover over a large area quickly. An unsightly shed, a large bare wall or similar structure will soon be lost behind its leafy mantle. From July to autumn, too,

Pyracantha coccinea lalandei is a vigorous firethorn which can be as much admired from inside as out when it is trained around a window. The bright orange berries are preceded by a multitude of creamy-white flowers

this deciduous climber bears freely its pinkish-white flowers which are not without their beauty. Altogether this is a useful shrub to remember – but only plant it where it can be given its head and the site is in keeping with its growth potential.

Pyracantha (Firethorn). For a description of these very useful wall shrubs turn to p. 63.

Rosa (Rose). If we want to introduce vertical colour into our gardens we have, of course, a treasure chest of good things in the climbing and rambling roses. I shall content myself now with mentioning a few of these roses which I consider especially noteworthy (see p. 88 for a larger selection). The catalogues of rose specialists will provide information on many more which may be nearer your own tastes and requirements. The range of offerings is so great that, when making a choice, personal preferences must come into the picture more than they do with most shrubs.

For house walls the most suitable roses are the modern repeat-flowering climbers and climbing shrub roses like the grand old rose-pink, fragrant Zéphirine Drouhin and the primrose-yellow Mermaid, also fragrant and with showy deep yellow stamens which, once established, provides a lovely display of colour from early summer to autumn. Among ramblers, so excellent for pergolas, fences, pillars and arches, names like Paul's

Scarlet Climber, Albéric Barbier (yellow in the bud and then creamy-white), American Pillar (rose with a white eye) and Albertine (deep pink marked salmon in the bud and later coppery-pink) are legion.

Russian Vine, see Polygonum

Schizophragma. A handsome plant which resembles *Hydrangea petiolaris* (described on p. 71) is burdened with the name *Schizophragma hydrangeoides.* The generic name refers to the curious splitting of the seed capsules and the specific name to the hydrangea-like flowers. It is, however, the pale yellow bracts surrounding the small creamy-white flowers in July which are the chief attraction of this deciduous shrub. It will grow in semi-shade or sun, but usually flowers more freely in sunny positions. It will climb to 20 ft (6 m) or more once established.

Stauntonia. The evergreen, twining *S. hexaphylla,* which grows vigorously in milder districts, also reaches a height of 20 ft (6 m) or more. It has large leaves and white, tinged violet, fragrant flowers, and it deserves to be better known and more often grown.

Trumpet Creeper, see Campsis

Vine, see Vitis

Virginia Creeper, see Parthenocissus

The true Virginia creeper, *Parthenocissus quinquefolia,* a climber which colours brilliantly in autumn

Vitis. The genus *Vitis* includes the magnificent *V. coignetiae,* a strong-growing species with leaves often as much as a foot across. These colour superbly in the autumn. For covering a wall facing in any direction or adorning a large tree this vine can be thoroughly recommended – but it needs space to do it justice. There is magnificent autumn colour, too, from *V. vinifera* Brandt, a variety of the edible grape, whose leaves turn to lovely shades of red and orange at that time of the year. *V. v. purpurea,* called the Teinturier grape, is also notable in this respect for the claret-red foliage turns to a particularly striking shade of purple in the autumn. Both varieties need a warm south- or west-facing wall and will reach a height of 10 ft (3 m) or more.

Winter Sweet, see Chimonanthus

Wisteria. The wisterias are perhaps the best known of all climbing plants for their striking trails of flowers can hardly be overlooked in early summer. Superb wall plants, they are also much used, of course, for pergolas, pillars and similar structures and are sometimes grown as free-standing specimens on a short 'leg'. The most usually grown species is *W. sinensis,* a Chinese wisteria with mauve flowers borne on racemes up to a foot in length. Also handsome and popular is *W. floribunda macrobotrys* which has bluish-purple flowers borne on racemes up to 3 ft (1 m) long. There is also a very attractive white form, *W. floribunda alba,* with extra long racemes.

The delicate mauve flowers of *Wisteria sinensis* are produced from its twisted branches in May and June

Hedging Plants for Colour

Most gardens have a hedge of some sort to form a boundary, to provide a windbreak or maybe to afford some privacy. It is a permanent feature, yet so often little thought is given to making a hedge a really attractive and colourful part of the garden. There is, nowadays, a wide range of plants which are suitable for this purpose, either for a high hedge or for a low hedge forming a division within the garden or alongside a path. For the last mentioned purpose, of course, the fragrant lavender has much to commend it.

Privet which was planted in suburban gardens in vast quantities years ago is deadly dull and impoverishes the soil so thoroughly that it should never be planted in a small garden. While the golden form is more cheerful looking it is an equally hungry plant. As I have already said a hedge is a permanent feature, so give considerable thought to the subject before deciding which plant will be most suitable to meet your requirements, always bearing in mind the kind of soil available and the aspect.

Preparing the Soil

The next thing is to prepare the soil thoroughly, for once the hedge is planted there is not much that can be done, other than an occasional topdressing with leaf-mould or peat, if it should prove necessary. If the depth of soil permits it should be dug to a depth of about 18 in (45 cm), but the subsoil must not be brought to the surface. Dig a trench, at least 2 ft (60 cm) wide, and having taken out the top soil, break up the subsoil with a fork to ensure good drainage, before replacing the top soil. When this soil is being put back into the trench, work in some well-rotted farmyard manure, if obtainable, or failing this some hop manure and garden compost. Bonemeal, applied at the rate of 4 oz to the square yard (110 g to the square metre), is also a good slow-acting fertilizer. Quick-acting fertilizers should be avoided where hedges are concerned. If the soil is deficient in lime then fork in, or scatter on the surface,

hydrated lime at the rate of up to 4 oz to the square yard (110 g to the square metre). Remember, however, that such plants as the common, purple *Rhododendron ponticum,* which makes quite a good evergreen hedge, requires a lime-free soil.

There should be a gap of at least some weeks – the longer the better – between the preparation of the soil and planting so that the soil has time to settle.

Planting

I prefer to plant deciduous hedges in the autumn, although any time from mid-October to mid-March is quite suitable, as long as the soil is in workable condition. Evergreen hedges are best planted in September or October, or from mid-March to early May. One must remember that evergreens never cease to lose moisture through their leaves and they are, therefore, in a particularly vulnerable position until they have established themselves in their new home. Where evergreens are planted in the spring and the weather becomes dry and warm, the plants will benefit from a spray overhead with water in the evenings until they have made new roots and become established. This attention has saved many a gap in a young hedge and is well worth the effort. Cupressus and yew often give the most trouble in this respect. If a polythene bag is placed over each specimen for a week or two after planting this will prevent many losses.

Should there be a long dry spell of weather it will be necessary to water the plants thoroughly at the roots. Mulching with moist peat or compost around the plants will help to conserve moisture. Grass cuttings may also be used for this purpose so long as the lawn has not been dressed recently with selective weedkiller.

Size of Plants

Frequently a hedge is required to provide a screen as quickly as possible, and for this reason tall plants are

The purple beech, *Fagus sylvatica purpurea*, forms a dense, deep-coloured hedge and retains some of its leaves through the winter, even though they are crisp and dry to the touch

ordered. This, however, may not achieve the objective for such plants take longer to become established and may not have good fibrous roots, unless they have been regularly transplanted while growing in the nursery. Plants which have not been transplanted will probably have woody roots, and, while they may be cheaper in the first instance, should be avoided because they will take much longer to 'get away' and losses can be considerable, so that they may turn out to be an expensive proposition. Hedging plants are quoted by the 100 or in tens.

Some hedging plants, such as pyracantha and broom (cytisus), are grown in containers by nurserymen and can, therefore, be planted at almost any time so long as the ground is not frozen, and it is not high summer. Such plants cost more, of course, than those which are grown in large quantities in the open ground.

There are many good hedge plants, but some will not do well in all places. I have, therefore, made three lists, namely for town gardens, chalk soils, and the seaside, which are the most difficult situations. People who live in easier places should remember that shrubs for town gardens will grow in the country, and those for chalk soils will grow on lime-free soils, but those listed for the seaside will not necessarily grow inland, because frosts are generally much worse inland than by the sea. For ease of reference I have sometimes included the same plant in more than one list.

For Town Gardens

The following are all useful plants for this purpose:

Barberry, see Berberis

Beech, see Fagus

Berberis (Barberry). Three good evergreen hedging plants are *B. darwinii*, with orange-yellow flowers in April–May; *B. gagnepainii*, yellow, which flowers in the second half of May; and *B. stenophylla*, orange-yellow and April–May flowering. These will make hedges of 8 ft (2·5 m), 4 ft (1·25 m) and 10 ft (3 m) respectively.

Cotoneaster. The scarlet-berried *C. simonsii* with silvery-grey bark makes a good hedge of about 5 ft (1·5 m) in height.

Cupressocyparis leylandii. This fast-growing conifer makes a good hedging plant, see p. 65 for a description.

Euonymus. The evergreen *E. japonicus*, except in its interesting variegated forms, is not a very exciting shrub but it stands up well to atmospheric pollution and will provide a screen some 10 ft (3 m) in height. This is not a shrub for cold gardens, but is excellent in coastal areas.

Fagus (Beech). The popular beech, *F. sylvatica*, is almost as good as an evergreen for hedging for the leaves, which turn a lovely bronze colour in autumn, remain on the plants throughout the winter.

Firethorn, see Pyracantha

Flowering Currant, see Ribes

Forsythia. As a hedging plant, forsythia can be extremely attractive in spring. Chestnut fencing, for example, can be masked successfully with this shrub and the best-known variety undoubtedly is *F. intermedia spectabilis*, a rich deep yellow in colour, which will make a hedge up to 10 ft (3 m) tall.

Hebe. This is the correct generic name for the evergreen shrubby veronicas. The hardiest is *H. brachysiphon* (syn. *traversii*) which bears white flowers in June. This will make a hedge up to 6 ft (2 m) tall.

Holly, see Ilex

Honeysuckle, see Lonicera

Ilex (Holly). There are numerous varieties of the evergreen common holly, *I. aquifolium*, which make good hedge plants and screens up to 20 ft (6 m) tall if necessary. The elegant but slow-growing gold and silver forms, like *I. a.* Golden King and *I. a.* Silver Queen, are to be recommended.

Laurustinus, see Viburnum

Lonicera (Honeysuckle). The small-leaved evergreen *L. nitida* makes a neat formal hedge when carefully trimmed to a wedge-shaped top, this last being necessary to avoid the hedge being broken down by the weight of snow in winter. For a hedge with a height of about 4 ft (1.25 m) it has much to commend it, but remember that it can be damaged by severe weather. There is a golden form which is especially attractive.

Osmarea burkwoodii. This handsome evergreen with dark green foliage and fragrant white flowers in May makes a hedge about 5 ft (1.5 m) tall. It is certainly worth considering, especially if a good hedging plant is wanted which is rather out of the common run of things.

Pyracantha (Firethorn). The evergreen pyracanthas, so overplanted as wall shrubs in years past, are, of course, splendid shrubs and they make excellent informal hedges (if clipped few berries are borne). Best known is *P. coccinea lalandei* with bright red berries and *P. atlantioides* which will make fine hedges of 10 ft (3 m) or so in height, if required.

Rhododendron. Some of the rhododendrons make good hedging plants for lime-free soils. The common rhododendron, *R. ponticum* (height 7 to 15 ft [2.25 to 4.5 m]), grows well in towns and so do some of the named hybrids, which will make a most colourful screen but will also cost considerably more to buy.

Pyracantha watereri forms a thorny, impenetrable thicket and has the advantage of bearing creamy-white flowers in early summer and berries later in the year

Ribes sanguineum (Flowering Currant). The flowering currant and varieties such as King Edward VII make attractive hedges of 8 ft (2.5 m) or more in height within a garden, but are not thick enough for a boundary hedge. The rosy-red flowers of *R. sanguineum* appear in April and have a delightful foil in the bright green leaves. King Edward VII has deep crimson flowers.

Taxus baccata. A good hedging conifer, see p. 68.

Viburnum. An evergreen viburnum which is excellent for hedge making is the popular laurustinus, *V. tinus*. This makes a hedge up to 10 ft (3 m) tall and bears attractive clusters of white flowers – pink in the bud stage – during winter and spring. The leaves are dark green.

For Chalk Soils

Beech, see Fagus

Berberis. Numerous species and hybrids, both evergreen and deciduous, are useful for this purpose, including *B. darwinii, wilsoniae, stenophylla* and *thunbergii*.

Buxus (Box). The common box, *B. sempervirens*, is a fine evergreen hedge plant for chalky soils, providing screens of 8 ft (2.5 m) or a little more in height. There is a colourful gold-variegated variety named *aurea maculata*. For low hedges of 3 ft (1 m) or less in height there is *B. s. elegantissima*, which has leaves edged with silver, and the edging box, *B. suffruticosa*.

Chaenomeles (Japanese Quince). The numerous varieties of *C. speciosa* will provide hedges of heights from 4 to 8 ft (1.25 to 2.5 m). Especially attractive are the 5-ft (1.5 m) tall Knap Hill Scarlet, with flowers of orange-scarlet, and the apple-blossom pink Moerloosii, which grows to a height of about 6 ft to 7 ft (2 to 2.25 m). Prune back the shoots after flowering otherwise the plants are liable to sprawl.

Cherry Plum, see Prunus

Cotoneaster. Of the numerous evergreen and deciduous cotoneasters suitable for this purpose I would mention *C. lacteus*, an evergreen species which bears white flowers in June and red berries later and makes a hedge of about 10 ft (3 m), and the semi-evergreen *C. simonsii* with showy dark leaves which bears its red berries freely in autumn. This makes a hedge of up to 5 ft (1.5 m).

Cupressocyparis leylandii. See p. 65 for a description.

Escallonia. Deservedly popular as seaside shrubs, the hardiest of this genus of evergreens is *E. langleyensis* with light crimson flowers but none of them are reliable except at the seaside. Escallonias are best grown as an informal hedge or windbreak so that the arching sprays of flowers can be seen to full advantage. *E. langleyensis* makes a hedge of up to 10 ft (3 m), and varieties like the

One of the deciduous barberries, *Berberis thunbergii atropurpurea* will make an attractive, richly coloured hedge up to 6 ft (2 m) high. It is thorny and quite effective in keeping out unwanted animals

deep red C. F. Ball and the pink Donard Seedling screens of about 6 ft (2 m) in height.

Fagus (Beech). *F. sylvatica* is a good standby on chalky soil and the absence of flowers is made up for by the attractiveness of its leaves – fresh green in spring and bronze throughout the winter. It makes a hedge 5 to 10 ft (1·5 to 3 m) tall.

Firethorn, see Pyracantha

Fuchsia. Hardy fuchsias, notably *F. magellanica riccartonii*, with red and purple flowers, make charming hedges, especially within a garden, in mild districts. Height 4 to 8 ft (1·25 to 2·5 m).

Guelder Rose, see Viburnum

Japanese Quince, see Chaenomeles

Laurustinus, see Viburnum

Lavender, see Lavandula

Lavender Cotton, see Santolina

Lavandula (Lavender). Lavender makes a delightful small hedge for a sunny position and well-drained soil.

There are several varieties of the evergreen *L. spica*, the old English lavender, and *nana* Munstead Dwarf is one of the most compact, growing about 1 ft (30 cm) high. This has deep lavender-blue flowers.

Lilac, see Syringa

Myrobalan, see Prunus

Prunus. The myrobalan or cherry plum (*P. cerasifera*) makes a quick-growing hedge up to about 10 ft (3 m) and the small white flowers are attractive in spring. The varieties *pissardii* and *nigra* have dark purple leaves and make a striking background for white-flowered hardy herbaceous plants.

Pyracantha (Firethorn). The evergreen pyracanthas also make stout hedges and when grown informally, that is not clipped too vigorously, the berries – orange, red or yellow, depending on which species or variety is planted – are freely borne and are most colourful in autumn. Plant container-grown specimens about 1½ to 2 ft (45 to 60 cm) in height. These make a hedge 4 to 8 ft (1·25 to 2·5 m) tall.

Rosmarinus (Rosemary). On a light, well-drained soil the aromatic *R. officinalis* makes a delightful evergreen hedge up to 6 ft (2 m) tall. Trim after the blue flowers have faded in June.

Santolina. The evergreen lavender cotton, *S. chamae-cyparissus* (syn. *S. incana*) has silvery-grey leaves covered with white felt and during the summer bears yellow, button-like flowers. It makes an effective hedge for bordering a path, growing 1½ to 2 ft (45 to 60 cm) tall.

Senecio. If something taller with silvery-grey foliage than the santolina mentioned above is required, then plant *S. laxifolius* which grows 3 ft (1 m) tall and also provides an evergreen screen. The leathery leaves are covered with grey felt on the underside. In June and July it bears yellow, daisy-like flowers.

Snowball Tree, see Viburnum

Syringa (Lilac). Where a big, fast-growing screen is required the lilac, *S. vulgaris*, is most decorative. There are single and double varieties in shades of deep purple, mauve, rosy-pink and white, and, of course, the fragrance is enchanting. When grown as an informal screen – up to 10 ft (3 m) tall – the flower heads should be removed before they start to seed, at the same time thinning out weak growths. A hedge of this kind may be expensive initially but it makes an admirable, very hardy and lasting screen.

Taxus baccata. For a description see p. 68.

Viburnum. The laurustinus, *Viburnum tinus*, does as well on chalk as it does in town gardens (see p. 77). The guelder rose, *V. opulus*, makes a hedge up to 10 ft (3 m)

and bears flat heads of white flowers in June and red berries in autumn. The foliage also takes on pleasing autumn tints. The snowball tree, *V. opulus sterile*, can also be planted as a hedge and bears white balls of bloom in June. It makes a hedge of about 5 to 6 ft (1·5 to 2 m) in height.

For Seaside Gardens

Having a garden near the sea can be pleasant but it also presents problems. Frost is not usually one of these, but gales and salt spray can play havoc with many plants so they must be chosen with care, particularly where hedges are concerned as shrubs used for this purpose will

Hedges make effective backgrounds. Here, yew *(Taxus baccata)* forms an evergreen backcloth for an herbaceous border. The bright colours of the perennials stand out well against the sombre green

probably be exposed to all the elements. The following should prove satisfactory and provide colour or a pleasant foil for colour.

Atriplex halimus (Tree Purslane). This shrub is semi-evergreen with silver-grey leaves and though it cannot be described as colourful it withstands spray and gales like a seagull, and provides a useful foil and protection for tender and/or more colourful plants within the

Although they are not usually the first plants to spring to mind when choosing hedges, roses can make a superbly decorative screen – clipped or pruned lightly so that flowering is not too adversely affected

garden. Planted in a double row it will form a useful windbreak 6 to 8 ft (2 to 2·5 m) high.

Cherry Plum, see Prunus

Cupressocyparis leylandii. This very useful conifer, to-gether with its golden form Castlewellan, withstands coastal conditions well, see p. 65.

Escallonia. *Escallonia macrantha* is an especially good seaside shrub and will provide an evergreen screen up to 10 ft (3 m) high. It bears bright red flowers in June and July and has large glossy green leaves. Hybrids of this species also thrive by the sea.

Euonymus. Planted extensively along the south coast of England, *E. japonicus* has dark glossy green leaves that are usually unharmed by spray. The gold and silver forms, like *ovatus aureus* and *microphyllus albus*, are more decorative than the type. All these make hedges up to 8 ft (2·5 m) tall.

Fuchsia. A fuchsia that is often grown for hedging pur-poses near the sea in milder areas, is the red and purple flowered *F. magellanica riccartonii*. It makes a hedge of up to 8 ft (2·5 m)

Gorse, see Ulex

Hebe. The hebes, or shrubby veronicas (see p. 76 for description), provide a useful screen throughout the year.

Hippophae rhamnoides (Sea Buckthorn). This is another useful windbreak hedge plant with silvery leaves and bark and orange berries in autumn. To obtain berries, though, some male plants must be planted with female specimens.

Hydrangea. In the milder areas of the country, *H. macrophylla* and its many colourful named varieties flower exuberantly. These will form hedges some 6 ft (2 m) or so tall.

Laurustinus, see Viburnum

Myrobalan, see Prunus

Prunus. The myrobalan or cherry plum, *P. cerasifera* (see p. 78), grows well by the sea.

Sea Buckthorn, see Hippophae

Tamarix (Tamarisk). The deciduous tamarisks are especially associated with seaside conditions, the two best known ones being the pink *T. tetrandra* and the rosy-pink *T. pentandra*. Both make good windbreaks of 10 ft (3 m) or more in height.

Tree Purslane, see Atriplex

Ulex (Gorse). The tough, colourful gorse, *U. europaeus*, makes a splendid evergreen barrier of up to 5 ft (1·5 m) in height and the long-lasting flowers have a refreshing honeyed fragrance on sunny days. The double-flowered variety *plenus* gives a wonderful display in April and May with its rich golden-yellow blooms and makes a better, more dense screen than the type. It also has a rather more compact habit.

Viburnum tinus (Laurustinus). This evergreen winter-flowering shrub, already described on p. 78, provides a useful screen for the whole of the year.

Rose Hedges

A hedge of roses used within a garden, to screen the vegetables perhaps, can be most effective during the summer. In addition, some of the shrub roses have colourful hips in the autumn. The choice is wide and one's selection can be made from any good rose cata-logue. Floribunda roses are also colourful and three that are admirable for hedging purposes are Queen Elizabeth, Masquerade and Chinatown; likewise, the shrub roses Fred Loads and Kassel. The *rugosa* roses are also excellent, especially the variety Scabrosa with large mauvish-pink, single flowers and large hips at the end of the season. The planting of briars such as *canina, laxa* and *multiflora,* which are offered for this purpose, is not to be recommended.

Roses for Display

Some plants look well in mixture, but not roses. There is too much variation in height and habit for them to be really satisfactory in assortment. The most effective way to plant roses is in good blocks of one variety with adjacent varieties carefully chosen to give a pleasing harmony or contrast. Of course, in small gardens large blocks are impossible, but even if there is only room for a dozen roses all told I would sooner see these in one, two or at the very most three varieties, than all different.

Before the advent of vermilion and vivid orange varieties there was really not much problem about colour association with roses, but nowadays varieties like Super Star and Orange Sensation can clash with some crimson, red and pink roses. White can be the salvation here as with so many other difficult flower colours. A bed of Iceberg behind a bed of Orange Sensation will show it off to perfection and no one can be offended by it. Some of the softer yellows can also be used, and also coppery-pinks, but these need more care and it would be wise to get cut flowers of the fancied varieties, and try arranging them in the same vase before deciding to plant them side by side in the garden. Though roses can be moved even several years after planting if it turns out that rearrangement is necessary, they do not take it so kindly as some other shrubs – rhododendrons, for example, azaleas and camellias. So it is wise to get things right at the outset.

Best Type for Colour Display

When planning primarily for colour display the floribunda roses are to be preferred to the hybrid teas, because they produce far more flowers at a time. Good hybrid teas will give enough flowers for a week or so in June or early July to make a fairly solid display, but thereafter their flower production is liable to be patchy.

This is even more true of climbers, and even those that are said to be continuous flowering produce as a rule only a scattering of blooms at a time after their main flush. For real colour effect it may be better to depend on varieties such as Albertine, American Pillar and Paul's Scarlet Climber that really do give one tremendous display, and then to rely on other climbers to keep the colour going later.

Variations in Habit

One point seldom discussed is the habit of roses. As I have already said, it varies a great deal between varieties and can make or mar the effect of a bed. Ideally roses should branch freely and make plenty of foliage so that they cover the ground well at all times when they are in leaf. A lot of varieties fulfil these requirements, but there are plenty which are sparse in habit and in foliage, and some which need to be planted more closely than others because of their erect habit.

Hybrid Tea Roses

PINK AND RELATED SHADES

Ballet. This variety is of medium height and has large bluey-pink flowers.

Bonsoir. The peach-pink, very fragrant blooms are well shaped.

Gavotte. An advantage with this variety is its rose-pink colouring with paler reverse, which makes it a good mixer with many other colours. It makes a medium-sized bush.

Grace de Monaco. The pale pink, globular flowers hold their colour well and have good fragrance.

Lady Sylvia. This is a rose which shows up well in the autumn. It bears shapely blooms of light pink marked with yellow at the base.

Madame Butterfly. This pale pink variety which has blooms flushed with golden pink at the centre is especially good for heavy, cold soils. It is worth growing despite its age (it was introduced as long ago as 1920).

My Choice. Opening to pink with a buff reverse, the beautifully fragrant blooms of this excellent, vigorous rose are gold shaded with crimson in the bud.

Percy Thrower. I can recommend this namesake of mine for garden display and for cutting. This variety is rose pink in colour and the blooms are borne freely.

Pink Peace. This sport of the famous Peace has rose-coloured blooms and makes a smaller bush than its parent.

Silver Lining. This variety bears very shapely blooms of soft rose paling to white at the base. It is also deliciously scented.

Stella. This is another of those excellent roses whose colour is not too easy to define – cherry red on the edge of the petals and pinkish-cream or ivory in the centre. The blooms are long and shapely.

CARMINE AND RELATED SHADES

Eden Rose. The rose-pink blooms of this variety are of especially good quality but are not so numerous as one would wish. It has excellent fragrance.

Rose Gaujard. A notable feature of this rose is its ability to perform well in wet weather – which counters the somewhat controversial colour, magenta with a white reverse. It has a pleasant scent.

Wendy Cussons. This is another of those roses, like Rose Gaujard, which can be quite difficult to blend successfully with other varieties – its hard cerise colouring does not mix well with clear reds and yellows. But against that the blooms have the most beautiful shape, and it is well known for its ability to do well in bad weather. The best recommendation to its quality, though, is the fact that it has won the Royal National Rose Society's President's International Trophy.

RED

Alec's Red. One of the finest introductions of recent years, this is another variety to have won the R.N.R.S.'s President's International Trophy (for the best new rose of 1970). But more than that, it has achieved a notable double by also winning in 1969 the Henry Edland Memorial Medal for the most fragrant new rose of that year. The colour of the large blooms is cherry red.

Champs Elysées. This is a deep crimson variety, the blooms of which have an attractive velvety texture. An excellent rose for a massed display.

Christian Dior. Shapely scarlet blooms are borne on a bush of well above average height, and the young foliage is of coppery colouring. A splendid rose but rather prone to mildew attack.

Ena Harkness. An excellent red rose which is another having blooms of a velvety texture. They do, however, tend to hang their heads.

Ernest H. Morse. A tall-growing, turkey-red variety with pleasing fragrance which bears its blooms freely on stiff growths.

Fragrant Cloud. The winner of the R.N.R.S.'s Presi-

dent's International Trophy for 1964, this rose has large blooms of coral-red colouring and fragrance to match the name.

Incense. Delightful fragrance is a strong point of this velvety-red variety.

Josephine Bruce. This is a fragrant variety with especially shapely blooms, essentially blood red in colour with deeper shadings.

Lancastrian. This is a strong-growing variety which bears very fragrant and shapely red flowers on stiff stems. Certainly one to consider for the collection.

Madame Louis Laperrière. Another splendid variety with rich crimson blooms and delicious scent.

Papa Meilland. This is a variety of medium height with richly scented blooms of deep crimson and good shape.

Red Devil. A tall-growing, vigorous rose of bright red colouring with especially good foliage.

Uncle Walter. Very large blooms of red colouring and unusually good shape characterize this variety, together with especially strong growth.

Westminster. A tall and vigorous bicolor rose with excellent fragrance. The blooms are coloured deep cherry red with a yellow reverse.

FLAME AND VERMILION

Alexander. A tall-growing variety with orange-vermilion blooms and good dark green foliage.

Duke of Windsor. Nicely scented vermilion blooms and excellent deep green foliage make this a very desirable variety.

Mischief. Another splendid variety this, having deep pink flowers with orange on the outside of the petals and disease-resistant, coppery-coloured foliage.

Mrs Sam McGredy. This variety has been in gardens now for almost 50 years but it is still sought after for its bright coppery-orange and red flowers and reddish-bronze foliage. Moreover the shapely blooms are freely produced and are notably good in wet weather.

Super Star. This fine rose has one drawback and this is that the distinctive light vermilion colour of its blooms makes it difficult to associate with other varieties. The flowers are of medium size and well formed.

YELLOW TO ORANGE

Apricot Silk. A deep orange-yellow rose with pointed blooms borne on long stems.

Beauté. This apricot-yellow variety has shapely flowers which perform well in wet weather and leathery, disease-resistant foliage.

Colour Wonder. An orange-salmon variety with yellow reverse and attractive olive-green foliage. Rather small growing.

Elizabeth Harkness. A free-flowering rose with rich

A rose garden with a formal outline is here surrounded by informal plantings of trees and shrubs, which give the whole garden a natural feeling. The hybrid tea roses are successfully underplanted with violas

An excellent, full-flowered floribunda, Vera Dalton has flowers of a rich pink. The foliage is leathery and disease resistant and the plant is of compact growth

fragrance and creamy-buff blooms marked with rose at the centre.

Gold Crown. Tall growing and upright, this is a variety with clear yellow blooms which pale with age. The dark foliage is disease resistant.

Grandpa Dickson. This is an excellent rose with strong, upright growth which bears freely its fine lemon-yellow blooms with a little pink on the margins of the petals. The colour fades a little with age. The foliage is deep green and shiny.

Just Joey. A coppery-orange, red-veined variety which makes an upright bush of vigorous growth with bronze-green foliage.

King's Ransom. A fine bedding rose of medium size with golden-yellow blooms which are borne freely.

Lady Belper. The especially well-formed blooms are apricot in colour warming to a near orange shade at the heart. It is of medium size and has a spreading habit.

Peace. No introduction is needed for this classic rose with its large blooms which vary in colour from pale to deep yellow and have cerise-pink shading at the edges of the petals. Equally well known is its great vigour and the consequent need to allow it plenty of space.

Piccadilly. A delightful bicolor of orange-scarlet and yellow colouring which changes as the blooms age to pink and soft gold. The foliage is reddish when young and matures to dark green.

Spek's Yellow. A popular bright yellow with shapely blooms, very upright growth and good vigour. The foliage is dark green and shiny, and disease resistant.

Sutter's Gold. The shapely and fragrant light orange-yellow blooms are shaded deep pink.

Whisky Mac. This very popular, strong-growing variety has beautifully fragrant blooms which start off deep gold in the bud with a darker coloured reverse and open to bronze yellow and apricot.

SHADES OF BLUE

Blue Moon. In colour terms this is the nearest yet to a truly blue rose with its lilac-blue colouring; but it is much more a cool or unheated greenhouse variety than one for the garden. The blooms are well scented and it makes a bush of medium height.

Sterling Silver. This is a good garden rose with lavender-lilac blooms which are both shapely and

84

fragrant. It is a general favourite with the flower arranger.

WHITE

Frau Karl Druschki. This very vigorous variety dates back to the first year of the century, but it is still worth growing. The large dead-white flowers have traces of pink on the outside. It is, however, rather prone to mildew attack.

Message. A splendid variety with pure white blooms borne on stiff stems – lovely viewed against the light green foliage. The buds, tinged with pale green, open well in all weathers.

Pascali. This variety has more resistance to mildew than most white roses and its blooms are very shapely.

Virgo. This is another white variety with very shapely blooms. They are borne freely and do not 'ball' in wet weather.

Floribunda Roses

PINK

Blessings. The hybrid tea-type blooms of this variety are of an appealing coral-pink shade. Another of its attributes is that it is very disease resistant.

Bridal Pink. Flesh-pink blooms are borne freely on a low, compact bush and have a good foil in the dark foliage.

Chanelle. This is an attractive rose with buds of warm amber colouring which open to China pink and cream but the colouring tends to become indeterminate with age. But it is a vigorous variety, covering the ground well, and seldom suffers from disease.

City of Leeds. An excellent gold medal variety which bears coral-flame blooms of hybrid tea type and performs well in all kinds of weather.

Dearest. Another gold medal variety of great charm with fragrant salmon-pink, flattish flowers with golden centres. However, the flowers, which are borne in large trusses, do not like wet weather, and this rose is not a success in Scotland.

Joybells. The rich pink flowers are of camellia shape and this variety makes a bush of medium size. Moreover, the good, glossy foliage is disease resistant.

Ma Perkins. A variety with strongly scented, double blooms of silvery-salmon colouring. It makes a medium-sized bush.

Pink Parfait. Freely produced on a compact, vigorous bush, the pale pink and orange blooms may be considered too delicate in colour for some tastes. Fragrance is not one of its strong points.

Queen Elizabeth. This fine variety is one of the best known of roses with its soft pink blooms, almost of hybrid tea quality, borne on very tall bushes. It makes an excellent hedge.

Spartan. A variety with double, cup-shaped blooms in rich salmon with the petals in the centre flame coloured. It is tall growing.

Tip Top. A useful rose for the front of the border with its compact growth and pleasing salmon-pink colouring. The blooms are of hybrid tea type.

Vera Dalton. The flowers of this variety, which does particularly well with me, are a delightful deep pink, bluer in shade than Dearest and more pointed in the bud, but opening cup shaped. The foliage is dark green and disease resistant and the growth compact.

Violet Carson. This is a rose of distinction with long, pointed, hybrid tea-type flowers which stand wet weather well. The colour is shrimp pink with a paler reverse and there is some fading with age. The flowers are well set off by the reddish-bronze foliage.

CARMINE AND RELATED SHADES

Daily Sketch. A bicolor with carmine-pink and silver flowers of large size. It is of medium height and makes bushy growth.

Paddy McGredy. The fragrant flowers of this hybrid tea-type floribunda are of cerise colouring and are borne freely. Not everybody's colour, perhaps, but a good rose of medium height and making a bushy plant.

Rosemary Rose. The highly distinctive blooms of this charming variety are rosette shaped – rather like those of a double camellia – and carmine crimson in colour. It is also vigorous and free flowering and has good bronze-red foliage. It is prone to mildew attack.

RED

Border Coral. A coral-salmon variety which bears its blooms in large trusses, and with colouring soft enough to associate with reds and the bright deep pinks. The growth is strong and spreading.

City of Belfast. A scarlet variety which has won the top rose award, the R.N.R.S.'s President's International Trophy (in 1967). With the attractive blooms go good foliage and disease resistance.

Europeana. This deep crimson variety has fully double flowers which are produced in abundance.

Evelyn Fison. The colour is almost geranium red and the petals are slightly frilled. With them go good dark foliage.

Happy Wanderer. Crimson-scarlet flowers are borne freely on low bushes. A good rose for the front of the border.

Lilli Marlene. This excellent rose has velvety crimson-scarlet flowers which are fully double and are carried in close clusters. It makes compact, bushy growth.

Marlena. A dwarf variety which bears its rich red flowers very freely. One of the best of the dwarf kinds now so popular.

Meteor. This is another dwarf variety of bushy habit with bright vermilion, semi-double blooms. It has little scent.

Paprika. Bright scarlet, semi-double flowers, a little lighter towards the centre. They stand up well to wet weather, and are produced freely. The foliage is shiny and dark green.

Red Dandy. This is a medium-sized variety with

scarlet-crimson blooms of velvety appearance and hybrid tea type.

Red Favourite. A compact variety with blood-red, semi-double blooms borne in large clusters over a long period. It holds its colour well, too, and is disease resistant.

Scarlet Queen Elizabeth. This has the splendid variety Queen Elizabeth as one parent and it makes a tall, up-right, vigorous bush. The flowers are orange scarlet in colour and are borne well into the autumn. An excellent border rose.

FLAME AND VERMILION

Anna Wheatcroft. This variety of medium height has reddish-salmon, semi-double flowers; also dark, healthy foliage.

Copper Pot. There is a delightful association of colour in this variety between the copper-orange blooms, more deeply coloured on the reverse, and the bronzy dark green foliage. It is a variety of medium size.

Highlight. This variety bears large trusses of orange-scarlet blooms, but as it clings on to its petals when the flowers are spent it can give an untidy effect. But it is vigorous and disease resistant.

Korona. Striking flame-scarlet, semi-double flowers make this a showy variety. It is strong growing.

Living Fire. This vigorous variety has bright orange colouring merging to scarlet and golden yellow at the base. It also has good, glossy, dark green foliage.

Orangeade. The deep orange colouring makes this a popular variety but I find that the blooms age to an un-attractive puce. The growth tends to be a little thin.

Orange Sensation. The hot orange red of this variety is not easy to mix with other colours, but it should be happy with a white floribunda like Iceberg. The flowers are double and produced in large clusters.

Orange Silk. This has orange-vermilion, double flowers of large size and is vigorous growing. A very good rose.

Topsi. A very free-flowering dwarf variety which has won the R.N.R.S.'s President's International Trophy (in 1972) and is extremely eye-catching with its mass of brilliant orange-scarlet, semi-double flowers.

YELLOW TO ORANGE

Alison Wheatcroft. The apricot-yellow blooms of this variety are flushed with crimson, becoming suffused with this colour all over as they age. It has glossy, dark green foliage.

Allgold. The great merit of this fine low-growing variety – it is only 2 ft (60 cm) tall – is that the golden-yellow blooms do not fade in sun or rain. It is also resistant to black spot and mildew.

Apricot Nectar. The blooms are shapely, apricot in colour and suffused with gold at the base. This medium-sized variety also has good foliage.

Arthur Bell. A very desirable variety with its excellent golden-yellow colouring and good scent. The shapely blooms are of hybrid tea quality.

Chinatown. This very strong-growing rose reaches a height of at least 5 ft (1·5 m) in good soil. It is an excellent variety with rich yellow, double flowers of hybrid tea shape borne in small clusters. The foliage is glossy.

Elizabeth of Glamis. The high awards the variety has won (the R.N.R.S.'s President's International Trophy and the Clay Vase, the top award for scent, both awarded in 1963) is an indication of its quality. The blooms are orange salmon and it is of medium height.

Golden Delight. This is another medium-sized flori-bunda with blooms of hybrid tea quality and deep yellow colouring. It is especially good in holding its colour in autumn.

Honeymoon. Canary-yellow, double flowers of large size carried until later in the autumn than the usual run of floribundas. It is tall growing.

Irish Mist. This is a vigorous grower with salmon-orange blooms of hybrid tea type.

Jiminy Cricket. The colour of this variety can be any-thing between salmon and pink, and it can be relied on to make a good show, even in wet weather. The foliage is reddish in colour.

Kerry Gold. The short stature and free flowering of this canary-yellow variety make it a good rose for the front of the border, especially as it combines good foliage with these characteristics.

Kim. Another low-growing floribunda, with bright yellow flowers, which is excellent for the front of the border.

Moon Maiden. An excellent variety with creamy-yellow flowers of large size, borne over a long period. The flower colour is well matched with the dark green foliage.

Woburn Abbey. A very showy rose with fragrant deep orange flowers of good size.

YELLOW AND OTHER SHADES

Masquerade. This is a popular rose dating back to the early 1950s which, however, is not to everybody's liking. It is interesting from the colour point of view because the flowers change from deep yellow to pink and then to deep red. Growth is vigorous and the foliage is disease resistant.

Redgold. Golden-yellow flowers suffused with rosy orange make this a showy variety and the dark, glossy foliage provides a nice foil.

Shepherd's Delight. The semi-double flowers are a mixture of yellow, orange and flame and the petals have frilled edges. It is a good rose in the autumn but tends to suffer from black spot.

LAVENDER AND RELATED SHADES

Africa Star. This rich mauve variety bears its flowers very freely over a long period, and is low growing. Its colour makes it especially useful for cutting for arrange-ment.

Lavender Lassie. This is a tall-growing rose with lilac-pink, rosette-shaped flowers with good fragrance.

Lavender Pinocchio. This variety has distinctive

greyish-lavender colouring and pleasing fragrance.

Lilac Charm. This is a pretty rose with its single, lilac flowers with their bosses of golden stamens. It is quite low growing and it has good foliage. It is also, understandably, very popular with flower arrangers.

BEETROOT PURPLE

News. The beetroot-purple colouring of this rose is unusually distinctive and it associates particularly well with floribundas of creamy-yellow colouring. It is a variety, too, of much interest to flower arrangers.

WHITE

Iceberg. A superb variety for garden display, its pure white flowers – flushed with pink in the bud – being carried with great freedom in largish trusses on a tall bush.

Isis. This white variety has hybrid tea-type flowers and dark green foliage.

Modern Shrub Roses

Ballerina. A hybrid musk shrub rose, up to 4 ft (1·25 m) tall, of unusual charm with its mass of single pale pink flowers with a white eye which are borne throughout the summer.

Bonn. The blooms of this vigorous 6-ft (2-m) tall variety are rose red suffused with vermilion.

Shrub roses associate particularly well with the herbaceous geraniums. Here the rose Constance Spry forms an excellent partner for *Geranium* Johnson's Blue which has tinted foliage in the autumn months

Constance Spry. The very fragrant *centifolia*-type blooms are of clear pink colour and are immensely attractive. These are borne only in midsummer on a bush of lax growth – it is usually best to support the growths – some 6 to 7 ft (2 to 2·25 m) tall.

Fountain. Blood-red flowers are borne with great freedom by this shrub rose, the first of its kind ever to win the R.N.R.S.'s President's International Trophy (in 1971). It makes a medium-sized bush.

Fred Loads. A very showy variety with its clusters of fragrant vermilion-orange, single flowers borne throughout the season. About 5 ft (1·5 m) tall.

Frühlingsgold. This fine variety produces its large golden-yellow to cream, semi-double blooms in May and June on arching stems. About 10 ft (3 m) tall.

Frülingsmorgen. This variety has pink, yellow-centred, single flowers with maroon-coloured stamens, but is in other respects like Frühlingsgold.

Golden Wings. A beautiful variety with large, pale canary-coloured flowers borne on a bush 5 ft (1·5 m) tall. The flowers are reminiscent of those of Mermaid.

Joseph's Coat. A very colourful rose, the double, golden-yellow and orange flowers flushed with cherry red at the edges are borne freely on a tall bush (it can also be grown as a semi-climber).

Kassel. This is a rose of hybrid musk origin with fragrant, deep cherry-red blooms borne in large trusses over an extended period. About 5 to 6 ft (1·5 to 2 m) tall.

Marguerite Hilling. This splendid variety is a rose-pink sport of Nevada (see below) which it very closely resembles in all but colour.

Nevada. This superb rose bears large, creamy-white flowers with golden anthers in June, sometimes again in August. It makes a shrub up to 8 ft (2·5 m) tall with attractively arched branches.

Nymphenburg. The fairly large, salmon-pink, gold-tinted flowers are borne on an upright-growing bush up to 6 ft (2 m) tall. It is nicely scented.

Scarlet Fire. This variety is a real asset to the garden in midsummer when the single, scarlet-crimson blooms with golden stamens are freely borne on a bush 6 ft (2 m) tall and through. There is a display of large red hips in autumn.

Will Scarlet. This is another 6-ft (2-m) tall variety with scarlet, semi-double flowers.

Climbing Roses

Autumn Sunlight. This variety produces its clusters of orange-vermilion flowers in abundance and gives a further display in autumn. Up to 10 ft (3 m) tall.

Casino. This recurrent-flowering variety has nicely fragrant, clear yellow, hybrid tea-type blooms which shade to lemon, and they continue until well into the autumn. 8 to 9 ft (2·5 to 2·75 m) tall.

Compassion. A recurrent-flowering variety with double, apricot-pink flowers which had the distinction of being the first rose of the type to win the R.N.R.S.'s Henry Edland Memorial Medal in 1973 for the most fragrant rose of the year in the Society's trials. Up to 10 ft (3 m) tall.

Copenhagen. This recurrent-flowering variety has bright red, fragrant blooms. 8 to 10 ft (2·5 to 3 m) tall.

Danse du Feu. Orange-scarlet flowers of medium size are produced in succession throughout the season. Suitable for north- and east-facing walls. About 8 ft (2·5 m) tall.

Galway Bay. This recurrent-flowering variety holds the colour of its pink flowers especially well. Up to 10 ft (3 m) tall.

Golden Showers. Large, fragrant yellow flowers. Recurrent flowering, this variety reaches up to 7 ft (2·25 m) tall grown on a pillar, more when against a wall.

Hamburger Phoenix. This recurrent-flowering, semi-double, scarlet-crimson rose is especially useful as it grows well on north and east walls. Up to 10 ft (3 m) tall.

Handel. A distinctive variety with its colouring of ivory shading to deep carmine towards the edges of the petals. The hybrid tea-type blooms are borne over a long period. Up to 10 ft (3 m) tall.

Inspiration. A salmon-pink recurrent-flowering variety with a deep carmine flush. It has especially shapely buds. Up to 8 ft (2·5 m) tall.

Meg. A very attractive recurrent-flowering variety with coral-salmon flowers, set off by bosses of golden stamens. Up to 12 ft (3·75 m) tall.

Mermaid. An outstanding rose with large, saucer-shaped, golden-yellow, single flowers. These are made more impressive by their prominent yellow stamens. The foliage is dark green and glossy. It grows vigorously once it has settled down, which may take a few years, and needs much space. The flowers are produced very freely. Up to 30 ft (9 m) tall.

Parade. This recurrent-flowering variety with carmine-crimson, fragrant blooms will grow well against a north or east wall. Up to 12 ft (3·75 m) tall.

Parkdirektor Riggers. A blood-red, recurrent-flowering rose which will grow well against a north wall, if the need arises. Up to 8 ft (2·5 m) tall.

Pink Perpetué. This very free-flowering variety has blooms which are pink on the inside, carmine outside. Up to 15 ft (4·5 m) tall.

Royal Gold. Recurrent-flowering and with hybrid tea-type blooms, this deep yellow variety is very attractive. Up to 10 ft (3 m) tall.

Schoolgirl. This coppery-orange recurrent-flowering variety has good fragrance and is especially suitable for growing on pillars.

Zéphirine Drouhin. This carmine-pink, almost double-flowered rose dates back over a hundred years and has thornless stems. It grows well on north-facing walls. Up to 12 ft (3·75 m) tall.

Rambler Roses

Albéric Barbier. Another good rose for a north-facing wall. The creamy-white, double flowers are borne in July and have a good foil in the shiny, dark green foliage. Young growth is coppery-purple, and the leaves are almost evergreen in mild winters. Very vigorous. Up to 20 ft (6 m) tall.

Albertine. A rampant-growing rose which produces its reddish to coppery-pink flowers with abandon in June and July. Up to 15 ft (4·5 m) tall.

American Pillar. This well-known rose has single rose-pink flowers with white centres and golden stamens which it bears in clusters in July. Very vigorous.

Paul's Scarlet Climber. Bright scarlet-crimson flowers are freely produced in small clusters. They are without scent. This is a strong-growing variety.

Sander's White. The trusses of fragrant, small white flowers are well set off by shiny foliage of light green colouring. Vigorous. Up to 15 ft (4·5 m) tall.

Wedding Day. The very fragrant flowers of this strong-growing variety are pale yellow in the bud, open white and become marked with pink as they age. They are borne in midsummer. The leaves are dark and leathery. Up to 30 ft (9 m) tall and a good variety for growing up a tree.

Mermaid is a climbing rose of exceptional beauty. Its single flowers are carried continuously throughout the summer and are deliciously scented. Although it is a strong grower and will eventually need plenty of space, it may take some years for it to settle down

Bulbs, Corms and Tubers for Colour

I find bulbous plants of all kinds a fascinating section of the plant kingdom. There is so much variety and they provide such opportunities for attractive display, formal and informal and in gardens large or small. Tulips and hyacinths are most effective for formal beds and a host of other plants, like daffodils and crocuses, are superb for informal planting, which I must admit is the kind I prefer.

I have said elsewhere in this book that I do not find tulips easy to place as they are too stiff and formal for my liking when planted in blocks of colour. I prefer to grow them individually or in small groups of one colour here and there. Mixing colours can be gay, but it brings its problems, for so often the heights of the different varieties vary, with the result that the bed looks uneven. With formal beds planting is usually done in straight lines, but this type of planting should be avoided wherever possible. Bulbs planted in regimented rows like soldiers on parade may look neat and tidy but it can easily be overdone. It is a different matter, of course, if bulbs are being grown for cutting purposes in, say, a part of the vegetable garden.

Plant in Good Time

A point to remember, particularly where dwarf bulbs are concerned, is to plant them in good time – in September or October, and the earlier the better. Such bulbs as dwarf narcissi, crocuses, *Iris reticulata*, muscari and scillas flower in the early spring and must be given time to make good root growth in the autumn to produce the best results in spring. These are all delightful when planted in small groups on the rock garden, or in some sunny corner where their early flowers will get some protection from the worst of the weather.

Late planting also means that the bulbs do not have sufficient time to make normal growth before the flower spike is produced and often the foliage is immature, which may mean that the second season's flowering will be disappointing. Gardeners have always got to look well ahead and must avoid making mistakes which may not become apparent for months, or in some cases years. First-class bulbs planted at the correct time should develop normally and give good results, but bulbs which have been lying about in bags for months at widely varying temperatures, in a dry atmosphere and planted late, may be a different story. Remember also to plant at the correct depth, for shallow planting is not satisfactory and may lead to the bulbs being damaged by frost.

Colour with Minimum Trouble

Here are some good kinds to provide colour with the minimum of trouble:

Allium. Not all ornamental onions possess the characteristic odour of the culinary varieties and those which do not are well worth growing for their striking flower heads. *A. moly*, the golden garlic, is a yellow-flowered species 12 in (30 cm) high which carries its many heads of flowers in June. It spreads well and can be used as ground cover. *A. ostrowskianum* is May flowering and bears 10-in (25-cm) stems topped by pink flower clusters. Plant the bulbs of both 3 in (8 cm) deep in October and November.

Anemone. For brilliant colouring the St Brigid and de Caen anemones are outstanding, in shades of crimson, dazzling scarlet, purple, blue and pure white. Plant the tubers 2 to 3 in (5 to 8 cm) deep in a moist, but well-drained soil and in a sunny position. September or October is the best planting time but in mild coastal districts the corms may be planted at any time of the year to provide a succession of flower over a long period. They range in height from 6 to 12 in (15 to 30 cm).

The early-flowering tuberous-rooted *A. fulgens* is a splendid sight on a rock garden in April and May when it produces its bright scarlet flowers on 12-in (30-cm) stems.

Bluebell, see Scilla

Chionodoxa (Glory of the Snow). Admirable for the rock garden or for naturalizing. The dainty clusters of blue flowers are produced on 6-in (15-cm) stems early in the year. Plant in the early autumn 3 in (8 cm) deep.

Crocosmia, see Montbretia

Crocus. The well-known, large-flowered crocuses should be planted about 3 in (8 cm) deep in well-drained soil in September or October. They are most attractive when planted in grass in clumps, or in a sunny position under trees. Once planted they may be left undisturbed for years. A point to watch when growing crocuses (or for that matter daffodils) in grass is that the grass should not be cut until the crocus leaves have died down, which is usually about the end of May. If they are to build up reserves of food which will allow them to flower well in the following year they must be allowed to complete their growth cycle.

In addition to the large-flowered hybrids there are several charming species, such as *C. tomasinianus*, with

In autumn and winter a pale pink carpet of *Cyclamen neapolitanum* brings life to the garden. Here, cyclamen accompany the taller flowers of *Crocus speciosus*

silvery-lilac flowers on slender stems in early spring. Once established this species will seed itself happily and make large colonies.

There are also autumn-flowering species which should be planted in July or early August, such as the bright blue *C. speciosus*, with vivid orange centres, and the rosy-lilac *C. zonatus* (syn. *C. kotschyanus*). These often increase by self-sown seed which takes about three to four years to flower when left undisturbed.

Crown Imperial, see Fritillaria

Cyclamen. There are various hardy cyclamen which flower in spring, summer or autumn, namely the carmine-flowered *C. coum*, the rosy-pink *C. neapolitanum* and the crimson *C. repandum*, among others. In addition, some such as *neapolitanum, europaeum* and *repandum* have most attractive mottled leaves which are still a delight in the depth of winter. Cyclamen corms should be planted in partial shade in a gritty, moist soil with plenty of leafmould and preferably some lime. Once they are planted they should be left undisturbed to seed themselves and form a colony. The corms should be pressed into the ground so that the top of the corm is only just covered with soil.

Daffodil, see Narcissus

Fritillaria. The majestic *F. imperialis*, commonly known as crown imperial, with its glossy green foliage and

The orange and yellow flowers of *Fritillaria imperialis* are borne on stately 3-ft (1-m) stems in April and tower above smaller inhabitants of the garden

drooping bells of orange, coppery-red or yellow, borne on sturdy stems 3 ft (1 m) or more in height in April, is a most imposing plant. The large bulbs should be planted about 6 in (15 cm) deep in September. They like a rich, deep soil. Choose a spot sheltered from the early morning sun, or the young growth may be damaged by frost. The bulbs and young growth have an unpleasant smell which is more than made up for by the lovely flowers. Check the price before ordering in any number, for the bulbs are expensive and not easy to come by.

The dainty flowers of *F. meleagris,* the snake's head, are carried on nodding 12- to 18-in (30- to 45-cm) stems in May. Several varieties are available, ranging in colour from white to mauve, and most have the characteristic chequered pattern on their blooms. Plant the bulbs in September.

Galanthus (Snowdrop). The common snowdrop, *G. nivalis,* is one of the earliest heralds of spring, its nodding heads of white and green coming as a delightful surprise in late January and February. There are also numerous other species and named varieties listed in good bulb catalogues. Plant the bulbs about 3 in (8 cm) deep in the early autumn and leave them undisturbed to form charming clumps. When it becomes necessary to lift and divide such clumps it is best done soon after they have finished flowering and while the foliage is still green, replanting immediately.

Galtonia candicans (Summer Hyacinth). *G. candicans* produces fragrant, white pendulous flowers in August and September on stems 3 to 4 ft (1 to 1·25 m) in height. The large bulbs should be planted in a sunny position about 6 in (15 cm) deep and left undisturbed for several years. October or March are the best months for planting. The plant is still listed as *Hyacinthus candicans* in some catalogues.

Gladiolus. There is now a great variety of gladioli to suit all tastes – large-flowered, dainty Butterfly types and many intermediate hybrids. The corms may be planted from mid-March until late April in well-drained soil and in a sunny position. Where the soil is heavy sprinkle a little sharp sand in the holes before planting the corms about 4 in (10 cm) deep. This sand, immediately beneath the corms, will improve the drainage and at the same time encourage root action. A little bonemeal will also prove beneficial. The corms are lifted in September or early October and after drying and cleaning are stored in a frost-free place for the winter.

Glory of the Snow, see Chionodoxa

Grape Hyacinth, see Muscari

Hyacinthus (Hyacinth). Fragrant hyacinths are delightful for window boxes or tubs, as well as for formal bedding schemes. Plant the bulbs in September, October or November about 3 to 4 in (8 to 10 cm) deep and about 6 to 8 in (15 to 20 cm) apart. In a sunny position beneath a window the colourful heads will be most welcome in the early spring. The blue *Hyacinthus amethystinus* with 6-in (15-cm) stems is most decorative on the rock garden in May.

Iris. The bulbous irises are quite distinct from the 'flag' or tall bearded irises which have perennial rootstocks. The first to flower are the dwarf species, such as *I. danfordiae* with deep lemon-yellow flowers on 3-in (8-cm) stems in January and February, and *I. reticulata* which bears its blue flowers in February and March. The Dutch, Spanish and English irises, which flower in that order, begin about the first week in June and continue in the case of the English varieties into July. They are grown in many gardens for cut flowers.

The Dutch and Spanish varieties should be planted about 3 in (8 cm) deep in the autumn. Plant the English irises about an inch deeper. In severe weather a top-dressing of peat or bracken will form a useful protection. All these irises like a sunny position and a well-drained soil with plenty of moisture during the growing season. They have stems about 2 ft (60 cm) in height. Plant *danfordiae* and *reticulata* in August–September 4 in (10 cm) deep.

The flowers of the iris, both bulbous and rhizomatous, are always a welcome sight in the garden for their colour and simplicity of form. There are many kinds to choose from and the Dutch irises, shown here, are among the first of the hybrid bulbous irises to flower

Leucojum (Snowflake). The snowflakes are taller and much larger than the snowdrops which they resemble somewhat. The first to flower in February and March is *L. vernum*, the spring snowflake, bearing large white bells tipped with green on 6-in (15-cm) stems. This is a delightful plant for naturalizing in groups. It is followed early in May by *L. aestivum*, the summer snowflake, which produces several flowers of a similar colour on stems about 1½ ft (45 cm) high. The bulbs of these two species should be planted in September or October, about 3 in (8 cm) deep. The little autumn snowflake, *L. autumnale*, should be planted in July or early August in a well-drained, sandy soil. In late September it produces nodding, white, pink-flushed flowers on slender 6-in (15-cm) stems. It is a charming but not spectacular plant. The snowflakes should be left undisturbed once they have been planted.

Lilium. The elegant genus *Lilium* comprises a great company of species and hybrids. They vary greatly in colour, height and habit, and, generally speaking, they are best planted in October or November, except on heavy soils where spring planting may be advisable. There are, however, exceptions, for the fragrant white Madonna lily, *L. candidum*, should be planted soon after it has finished flowering in July. Late August or September is the best period to move bulbs of this lily, which should be covered with only about an inch of soil.

Stem-rooting lilies should be planted 8 to 9 in (20 to 23 cm) deep (the easily grown white, flushed gold regal lily, *L. regale*; the orange tiger lily, *L. tigrinum*; the choice white, gold and red-spotted *L. auratum* and the white, crimson-spotted *L. speciosum* are some which fall in this category). The depth of planting will, of course, be governed by the type of soil in the garden, and in some cases the bulbs may have to be planted only about 4 in (10 cm) deep, topdressing later with leafsoil. As a general rule for other lilies 5 to 6 in (13 to 15 cm) is a satisfactory planting depth.

Montbretia. The montbretias are now botanically known as *Crocosmia*, but that does not make any difference to their cultivation, which is simple. The corms should be planted in March or April about 3 in (8 cm) deep in well-drained soil and in a sunny position. They increase rapidly, so should be planted at least 6 in (15 cm) apart. The slender, sword-like leaves are arranged like a fan and the graceful flower spikes in shades of orange, yellow and crimson appear in August and September. In exposed gardens the corms should be protected in severe weather with a layer of peat, bracken or straw.

Muscari (Grape Hyacinth). Flowering in early spring, the deep blue muscari are admirable for planting in little groups on the rock garden or for massing in the front of a border. Plant the bulbs in early autumn about 3 in (8 cm) deep and about 3 or 4 in (8 or 10 cm) apart. There is also a white form, and a plume-like variety, *M. comosum monstrosum*, which bears mauve, twisted flowers in May, some weeks later than most muscari.

Narcissus (Daffodil). The narcissi range from the tiny varieties suitable for the rock garden, naturalizing in grass or for growing in pans in a cold greenhouse, to the elegant and colourful hybrids which breeders in this country, and particularly in Ireland, have produced in ever-increasing numbers curing the past forty years or so.

Of the small species, perhaps the most widely grown are *Narcissus bulbocodium*, *N. cyclamineus* and *N. triandrus albus*. *N. bulbocodium* is known as the hoop petticoat daffodil and is ideal for naturalizing in grass. Its trumpets are very full and wide and are carried singly on 6-in (15-cm) stems in April. *N. cyclamineus* also looks well when planted in grass or a rock garden. Its lemon-yellow trumpets are long and narrow and its perianth segments reflexed. It is an early flowerer, carrying its nodding blooms on 4-in (10-cm) stems in February and March. *N. triandrus albus*, angel's tears, is an elegant species with creamy-white flowers carried on stems 6 to 9 in (15 to 23 cm) high. All three are planted in the garden 2 to 3 in (5 to 8 cm) deep in August, but the trumpet daffodils, the large-cupped varieties and many other large forms should be planted in September or October. Plant these with about 6 in (15 cm) of soil over the noses of the bulbs, or 4 to 5 in (10 to 13 cm) where the soil is heavy. Daffodils planted informally in groups under trees or in grassland are seen at their best. Bulb catalogues list varieties in a diversity of colours and forms sufficient to suit all tastes and pockets.

Ranunculus. The Turban or Persian Buttercup ranunculus make a gorgeous display in many brilliant colours in a sunny border in May and early June. Plant the tubers with the 'claws' downwards about 2 to 3 in (5 to 8 cm) deep in well-drained soil in February or March. They like plenty of moisture during the growing season and the tubers should be lifted in July and stored in dry sand in a frost-free place.

Scilla. The bluebells are listed in bulb catalogues under *Scilla*, to which genus they used to belong but have been moved to the genus *Endymion* by the botanists. The common bluebell and the various pink and white forms are delightful when planted in a wild or woodland garden. Plant in the autumn 2 to 4 in (5 to 10 cm) deep. The smaller Siberian squill, *Scilla sibirica*, is well suited for pockets on the rock garden where its dainty bright blue flowers on 4-in (10-cm) stems are a picture in March and April. Plant the bulbs about 3 in (8 cm) deep. This squill associates well with little clumps of dwarf narcissi.

Siberian Squill, see Scilla

Snake's Head, see Fritillaria

Snowdrop, see Galanthus

Snowflake, see Leucojum

Summer Hyacinth, see Galtonia

Tigridia (Tiger Flower). The brilliant Mexican tiger flowers (forms of *Tigridia pavonia*) are outstanding from July onwards when planted in full sun in well-drained soil, preferably in a sheltered corner of the garden. Plant about 3 in (8 cm) deep in April or early May, lift in October and store in dry sand away from frost for the winter. The flowers, borne on 18-in (45-cm) stems, are about 4 in (10 cm) across and are available in shades of glowing scarlet, bronze, orange and yellow with red-spotted centres and other variations. The flowers last only for a few hours but more appear each sunny day.

Tulipa (Tulip). Probably more tulips are planted than any other kind of bulb, with the exception of narcissi. The Early Single and Early Double tulips start to flower in April, followed in late April by the long-stemmed Mendel varieties. In the month of May there is a galaxy of Triumph, Darwin, Parrot, Rembrandt, Cottage, and Lily-flowered tulips, among other glorious types. By carefully selecting the varieties these tulips will give a brilliant display of colour for weeks on end.

In addition to these bedding tulips, there are the early-flowering tulips suitable for the rock garden, such as the striking *kaufmanniana*, *fosteriana* and *greigii* hybrids with exquisitely beautiful flowers. These flowers are borne on stems 6 to 8 in (15 to 20 cm), 1 to 1½ ft (30 to 45 cm), and 9 to 12 in (23 to 30 cm) tall respectively. Among the many species is the dwarf *T. praestans* from Central Asia which brings forth glossy vermilion-scarlet blooms in early April, as many as four on a branching stem. This species often causes considerable comment.

Several species produce more than one flower on a stem, and when modern hybrids do likewise it gives some indication of a cross made years ago by the plant breeders. It is not sensational and is unlikely to mean a fortune around the corner.

Plant tulip bulbs in October and November with about 4 in (10 cm) of soil above the nose of the bulb. The smaller bulbs of the rock-garden varieties may be planted a little less deep.

The large-trumpet daffodils or narcissi are seen at their best when naturalized in large drifts under trees. Here *Narcissus* Bermuda forms a golden sea of flowers underneath the early-flowering *Amelanchier lamarckii*

Rock Garden Plants for Colour

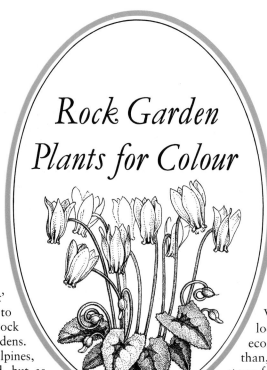

The term 'rock-garden plant' covers a great many plants used to provide colour and interest in rock gardens, dry walls and sink gardens. These plants are also called alpines, another term not readily defined, but as a general rule one must be careful not to use on the rock garden those plants which grow too large or are liable to become invasive. He is a clever gardener, however, who always places his rock plants in the right place, whether from the viewpoint of size or colour, but mistakes in planting provide useful experience. In any case I believe that the gay clash of, say, violet aubrieta and yellow alyssum is acceptable for a brief period after the drabness of winter. Always aim to have the colours well mixed and the interest spread over as long a period as can be arranged.

The rock-garden specialist frowns on the use of annual and biennial plants and would not dream of using gazanias, mesembryanthemums, dwarf antirrhinums and other summer-flowering plants to fill gaps, but if such plants give us pleasure in our own gardens let us enjoy them.

Site and Preparation

A rock garden should be in an open, sunny position away from overhanging trees. Ideally a south- or south-west-facing slope with thoroughly well-drained soil is desirable, for while rock plants like plenty of moisture during the growing season, many of them detest winter wet. In their mountain homes they are for months protected by a deep, crisp layer of snow which keeps the plants dry and at an even, if low, temperature. Obviously we cannot provide such winter conditions, but we can do our best to provide good drainage. If we have unusual and favourite plants these can be given protection from excessive winter rains by using small cloches, or just a sheet of glass supported over the plant by a piece of stout wire. The keen gardener will adopt ingenious methods to protect his treasures.

Construction

Where suitable stone is available locally it is far better and more economical to make use of it, rather than, for instance, transporting limestone from the Lake District to a Sussex garden, where the local warm-looking sandstone would be much more in keeping with the surroundings. Large flints or lumps of broken concrete are sometimes used for reasons of economy, but they do not weather readily and it is best to avoid them whenever possible.

If the rock garden is on a level site and the soil is heavy, it will be wise to make some provision for drainage before starting to place any stone. If a deep hole is dug and filled with coarse rubble this will drain away surplus moisture, and a layer of coarse ash or shingle just above and around the top of the soakaway will improve the drainage over the whole area of the rock garden. Where the rock garden is on a natural slope there should be no need for such work. Wherever the site is, it should be dug over and all perennial weeds carefully removed, otherwise they may become established beneath the rocks and can be extremely troublesome.

When placing the stones try and form natural-looking strata, and avoid placing pieces of rock on end – they will look like almonds decorating a cake. Ample sifted soil will be required to use around the pieces of rock, and the soil must be rammed firmly behind and around each piece.

Planting

When the construction work is completed do not start planting immediately, but wait for a week or two for the soil to get settled. It is best for the amateur to begin with a collection of plants that are easily grown and to make a selection which will provide colour and interest over as long a period as possible. (The general advice given on the use of colour in Chapter One should prove helpful at this time.) Later, when these have become established, try a few of the more difficult alpines which may be particularly interesting to you.

Rock plants are grown in containers by nurserymen and should be planted firmly. For this reason it is wise to let the soil settle on a newly-made rock garden before planting. If the ball of soil is very full of roots, press the soil gently and loosen the roots at the bottom, removing the 'crocks' if there are any among the roots at the bottom. With a trowel make a hole deep enough to take the roots without having to bunch them up, then gently but firmly fill in around the ball with fresh soil, leaving the neck of the plant level with the surface soil.

Suitable shrubs can be used to give height and depth to the top of a rock garden, while trailing and prostrate plants hug the ground between rocks to provide rivers of colour. Pink aubrieta, yellow cytisus, erica, rhododendron, deutzia and a pink-shooted pieris are used here

Propagation

Alpine plants can be increased by sowing seed or by taking cuttings. Named varieties of aubrieta, helianthemum and the like will not come true to colour from seed, and must be increased by cuttings. These are made from young non-flowering shoots, up to about 2 in (5 cm) long. Remove the lower leaves and with a sharp knife or razor blade make a cut immediately beneath a leaf joint. Insert the cuttings into pots, pans or a propagating frame containing moist sharp sand or a very sandy loam. Water them in and then stand them in a shaded frame and spray them overhead with water occasionally, using a fine syringe. These cuttings do not require heat and can be taken in the early spring, or later in the year soon after the plants have been trimmed back after flowering.

February is a good month to sow alpine seeds, although if you have saved seed from your own primulas

this should be sown as soon as it is ripe during the summer, and it will germinate quickly in cool, moist conditions. Seeds of alpines should be sown in pans or boxes containing a gritty, well-drained compost and these only require the lightest covering with sifted soil. Water carefully with a can fitted with a fine rose, then cover the pans or boxes with sheets of asbestos, or glass and brown paper, to exclude the light, and stand in a cold frame or cold greenhouse to germinate.

Some alpine plants lend themselves to division – armeria, sedum, sempervivum, some campanulas and dianthus, for instance. This can be done carefully in the spring or autumn and the small pieces which are removed with a little root should be potted singly. They should be kept in a cool, shaded frame for a week or two until they are established.

Choice of Plants

If your soil is naturally alkaline, that is if it contains lime or is chalky, there are certain plants to avoid, unless separate pockets of lime-free soil are made on the rock garden. This, however, is not always satisfactory, due to water containing lime seeping through and contaminating the soil. Plants which do not tolerate lime include rhododendrons (some of the dwarf species are charming for the rock garden), hardy heathers (other than the winter-flowering *Erica carnea* and its varieties), lithospermums, the bright blue, autumn-flowering *Gentiana sino-ornata* and its hybrids, and lewisias, which in any case are not plants for the beginner, and do best in or on top of a dry wall.

A good alpine nursery would be happy to supply a collection of, say, 50 different varieties of rock plants suitable for the beginner. Depending on the size of the rock garden you could have two or three plants of each variety and plant the varieties in groups. This will prove more effective than single plants dotted around. Such a collection should include armerias, named varieties of aubrieta, campanulas, dianthus, the creamy-white-flowered mountain avens (*Dryas octopetala*), geranium species, helianthemums (sun roses), *Phlox subulata* and its hybrids, potentillas, saxifrages, sedums, sempervivums (houseleeks), fragrant thymes, and various veronicas.

Plants for Special Purposes

Shade

A shady rock garden can be a problem but the following plants will do quite well: *Anemone nemorosa* and its varieties, the delightful little creeping dogwood, *Cornus canadensis*, with white, petal-like bracts, hardy cyclamen, *Daphne blagayana* with creamy-white fragrant flowers, the purplish-rose dog's tooth violet (*Erythronium dens-canis*), the blue *Mertensia virginica* and

Annual salvias, centaurea and alyssum add colour to the edge of the author's rock garden. The sink garden acts as a focal point above the rock pool

When planted up the rock garden should show a good balance between stone and plants

Omphalodes verna, pulmonarias in variety, the lilac-blue *Ramonda myconi* and the pink *Saxifraga umbrosa* (London pride) and its varieties.

Poor Soil

Where the soil is poor and plants are required that need little attention, a selection of the following should provide the answer: acaenas, ajugas, armerias (thrift), epimediums, erinus, the golden-yellow *Euphorbia myrsinites*, festuca (ornamental grasses), helianthemums in colours from yellow and orange shades to deep red, the red *Polygonum vaccinifolium*, the apricot and crimson blotched *Potentilla tonguei*, the pink *Saponaria ocymoides*, sedums (stonecrops) and sempervivums in variety, *Thymus serpyllum* and its varieties in shades of pink, mauve and white, *Veronica filiformis*, blue, and vinca (periwinkle).

Chalk Soils

Where the soil in a garden is lime or chalk the following plants will thrive: achilleas, aethionemas, alyssum, anemones, armerias, campanulas, dianthus, *Dryas octopetala*, *Erinus alpinus*, erodium, hardy geranium species, *Gypsophila repens*, helianthemums, hypericum, iberis, *Leontopodium alpinum* (edelweiss), linum (flax), oenothera, *Phlox subulata* and its varieties, saxifrages, scabiosa, sempervivums, and thymes.

Plants With Decorative Foliage

We must not forget the useful range of plants that have decorative foliage when other plants have finished flowering, namely *Achillea tomentosa*, *Artemisia lanata*, *Dryas octopetala*, epimediums, *Helichrysum marginatum*, *Sedum spathulifolium*, sempervivums, those

A small rock garden can be made in a sink or trough if space is limited. Here an old stone sink is planted with sedums, saxifrages, sempervivums and other alpines

colourful dwarf shrubs *Berberis stenophylla semperflorens* and *B. thunbergii atropurpurea nana*, and the many and varied dwarf conifers.

Bulbs and Corms for the Rock Garden

Bulbs are, of course, a delight not only in the spring but almost throughout the year if planted from the following selection: allium (decorative members of the onion family), chionodoxa, crocus (winter, spring and autumn flowering), the hardy cyclamen (spring, summer and autumn flowering), galanthus (snowdrop), *Iris reticulata* and other dwarf species, leucojum (snowflake), for spring and autumn, muscari (grape hyacinth), dwarf narcissi, puschkinia, scilla (squill), dwarf tulips, and for a warm, sunny corner, the zephyr flower, zephyranthes.

Sink Gardens

Where space is restricted alpine plants may be grown in old stone sinks or troughs and can be a charming feature on a roof or patio garden, providing colour and interest out of all proportion to their size. And, of course, in more spacious surroundings too they can add much to the overall picture, if carefully sited and planted.

Such sinks must have a drainage hole with a layer of crocks or shingle on the bottom. Cover this drainage material with a layer of leaves or rough peat and then fill to within about an inch of the top of the sink with a well-drained gritty compost. The soil may or may not have to be lime-free, depending on what plants are to be grown. The sink should be at least 6 in (15 cm) deep. The larger and deeper the better, for a sizable trough will not dry out so quickly in hot weather. It should be stood in an open, sunny position and if it is possible to stand it on a stone pillar or balustrade at about eye level it will be more easily admired.

A few pieces of stone – tufa is very suitable – can be used but do not overdo the stone or there will be little room for plants. This rock garden in miniature should have a sprinkling of stone chippings scattered around the plants as a finishing touch. This will not only assist drainage around the collar of the plants but will also deter weeds. Be careful not to use limestone chippings if the plants are intolerant of lime. Do not use rampant plants such as many of the sedums and the stronger growing houseleeks, and remember that miniature roses do not as a rule live long when planted in sinks. Plants that do thrive are the rose-red *Aethionema* Warley Rose, the rose-pink *Androsace sarmentosa* (to trail over the edge), the white to pink *Armeria caespitosa*, the blue *Campanula cochlearifolia* (syn. *C. pusilla*), the rose-red *Dianthus alpinus* (which likes lime), *D. neglectus* (which does not like lime) of similar colouring, the violet-purple *Erinus alpinus*, the yellow *Iris pumila*, the golden-yellow *Morisia monantha*, *Phlox douglasii* and its varieties in various colours, Kabschia varieties of saxifrage, and the small, compact *Sempervivum arachnoideum*. The little Noah's Ark juniper, *Juniperus communis compressa*, is a very slow-growing conifer which is admirably suited for a miniature rock garden.

Once planted a sink garden requires little attention other than hand weeding occasionally and watering in dry weather. Where the sink is large enough a few small bulbs, such as miniature narcissi and the smallest crocuses, may also be planted.

Dry Walls

A dry wall in a garden can be made a colourful feature by planting suitable rock plants between the horizontally laid stones. A dry retaining wall is one that is constructed without the use of cement, and rectangular pieces of sandstone are often used for this purpose. The warm golden colour of this stone makes a pleasing background for rock plants, and is not so hard or cold-looking as granite which is extensively used for walling, instead of hedges, in northern areas of England. Nevertheless granite is most durable and is rarely damaged by frost, so if this stone is available locally use it by all means. It will look more in keeping than transported stone of an entirely different nature. It is, however, more difficult to lay being usually of odd, boulder-like form, rather than rectangular.

A retaining wall has soil behind it, that is, it is built to support soil on a sloping site, and between each layer of horizontal stones is placed about an inch or so of soil, instead of mortar, in which plants will grow happily. Ideally the planting should be done as the wall is built, but in practice this seldom seems to happen. There is, of course, a limit to the height of a wall which is not bound together with mortar, and the higher the wall the broader must be the base. The face of the wall should be gently inclined, not vertical. This slight angle will keep the soil moist between the horizontal stones, and, with a row of large pieces among the top, sloping inwards, rain water will get to the plants' roots in the soil behind the walling.

An attractive feature can be made by constructing a rectangular island site with a surrounding retaining wall, say 2 ft (60 cm) in height, and filling this with soil. This will then provide not only a sunny side, but also a shaded side suitable for those alpines that will not flourish in hot sun. The top of the island can be planted as a scree for rock plants that like sun and good drainage, as well as small bulbs – dwarf narcissi, crocuses, miniature irises, scillas and tulip species – and a selection of dwarf conifers, which are so charming throughout the year.

Whatever type of garden wall is constructed, even a wall made of peat blocks (which can be a charming feature for peat-loving plants), it is important to make sure that the foundation is properly prepared. Start by taking out a shallow trench and into this put a layer of old ashes, pebbles or similar material to provide drainage. Over the drainage material put inverted turves or coarse peat and then start the first row of stones, which should be large and about 3 in (8 cm) below the surface soil. This will give a firm base upon which to build the wall.

Suitable Plants

Sunny Walls

A sunny dry wall can be a very warm spot so choose plants that enjoy such conditions. Some of these are, of course, suitable for the rock garden also, and have already been mentioned. Suitable plants are the rose-coloured *Acantholimon glumaceum*, the summer-flowering *Aethionema* Warley Rose with many heads of rose-pink flowers on sturdy little stems, the various alyssums and arabis, the long-flowering, pink adrosaces with attractive rosettes of grey, hairy leaves, aubrietas, in shades of mauve, lavender, pink and deep red, and campanulas and dianthus in variety. Sun roses (helianthemums) flower throughout the summer and present no difficulty. If they are trimmed back as soon as the flowers start to fade a second crop will often be produced. Clipping also keeps the plants bushy. There are many different named varieties in shades of orange, copper, yellow, glowing red and pink. An old favourite of mine is *H. apenninum roseum*, with clear pink flowers and ash-grey little leaves.

Another easy plant is the mountain avens, *Dryas octopetala*, which forms a close dark green mat of attractive leaves and bears large white flowers with prominent gold centres in early summer. It will grow in the poorest soil and likes full sun. Other colourful plants are *Iberis sempervirens* (perennial candytuft which has several named varieties); lewisias; *Lithospermum* Heavenly Blue; *Phlox subulata* in variety; *Polygonum vaccinifolium* with erect spikes of deep pink flowers in late

Raised rock beds are an ideal way of creating more space in a small garden. Many plants, including more difficult alpines, appreciate such growing conditions

summer and autumn; *Saponaria ocymoides*, a trailing soapwort with bright pink flowers; many kinds of houseleek (sempervivum) and sedums; forms of *Saxifraga aizoon*, and *Veronica prostrata* in variety. For a really well-drained, sunny corner the Californian fuchsia, *Zauschneria californica*, makes a fine splash of scarlet in the late summer and autumn. The foliage is grey which adds to the attraction.

Shady Walls

Hardy ferns, such as the little *Asplenium trichomanes* with elegant green 6-in (15-cm) fronds borne on black, shiny stems, are excellent for this purpose. Where it is moist as well as shady the common primrose makes a charming feature and some of the other dwarf primulas can be planted. The little *Hutchinsia alpina* forms a close mat of green covered in spring with dainty white flowers. The navel wort, *Omphalodes cappadocica*, has erect stems about 9 in (23 cm) high bearing forget-me-not-like blue flowers during the summer, and the closer-growing ramondas are admirable for a cool, north-facing crevice. The species from the Pyrenees, *Ramonda myconi*, has sprays of lilac-blue flowers, resembling that of the potato but on 3-in (8-cm) stems. With a selection of these and many other plants, not forgetting small bulbous plants for the top soil of a retaining wall, even quite a small stretch of walling can be a delightful and interesting feature in a garden.

Plants for Paved Areas

A paved terrace, patio or path is a permanent feature in a garden, and while the initial outlay may seem heavy, there is neither the upkeep nor the mowing that grass requires to be kept in good condition. A terrace or patio, moreover, can be used as a sitting-out area almost immediately after rain and it can be made very bright and colourful indeed by planting suitable plants between the stones. Such areas, too, are ideal sites for stone sinks containing rock plants (see p. 100) and other containers providing homes for many different plants (see p. 120). Paving is far more satisfactory than grass for a path that is going to have regular use, particularly near the house where grass can become worn in the summer and muddy in the winter.

The rock-plant enthusiast will make up his mind that paving offers him opportunities to grow many attractive plants between the intersections of the stones, either in formal rectangular paving or even more so in random or crazy paving. Where planting is done between rectangular paving, it will probably be necessary to chip the corners of the stones to make a space for the plants. A fern trowel is a useful tool to remove some of the soil, ash or sand on which the slabs have been laid, and this is replaced with a little gritty potting compost in which the rock plants will quickly make roots.

Few plants will endure being trodden upon frequently, so do not overdo the planting in the middle of the path but concentrate mainly on the sides. Choose low-growing carpeting plants or those of neat, bushy habit. It is not advisable to introduce plants in a path where it happens to run beneath trees, because the plants will not usually flourish, and in addition they may all too often become slippery due to drip from overhanging branches.

Nurserymen grow rock plants in pots and this means that they can be planted at almost any time except when the ground is frozen. When planting make the soil firm around the ball of roots, and should the pot-grown plant be root-bound, loosen the soil around the lower roots, removing any crocks that may happen to be in the soil so that the roots will quickly become established in the new soil. Then water the plants with a can fitted with a fine rose, and should the weather be dry water daily until the plants have happily settled in.

Where a path is in the shade on the north side of a house, or beneath overhanging trees, the stone slabs can become dangerously slippery in wet weather. If the stones are brushed over with a solution of domestic bleach this will usually cure the trouble, at any rate for a time, but do not saturate any plants with the solution. It is unlikely, however, that there will be plants growing in a path with such an aspect.

Some Planting Suggestions

The following plants are suitable for planting between the intersections of paving stones and will make a pathway both interesting and colourful: acaenas, compact varieties of armeria (thrift), *Achillea prichardii, Anthemis nobilis* Treneague, a non-flowering chamomile which forms a dense green mat; and aubrietas, in shades of mauve, lavender, pink and red, and dwarf forms of dianthus, all of which like a well-drained, sunny position.

Then there is the minute white daisy, *Bellium minutum; Erigeron mucronatus* with white and pink flowers from spring until autumn; dwarf campanulas, such as *C. cochlearifolia* (syn. *C. pusilla*) with dainty little bright blue bells on 3-in (8-cm) stems, and the spreading *Dryas octopetala* with dark green leaves and most pleasing large, creamy-white flowers with golden centres which are freely produced in early summer. *D. octopetala* is easily raised from seed, in fact, in some gardens self-sown seedlings appear in gravelly soil.

Plants which appreciate dry and sunny situations will grow well in the crevices of steps and paving. Plants such as thyme smell delicious when they are walked on — though continuous trampling can wear them out

Dwarf conifers of an upright habit lend height and background colour to a group of low-growing plants. *Thuja orientalis elegatissima* **is seen in the foreground**

The grey-green tufty grass, *Festuca crinum-ursi* (syn. *F. eskia*) is decorative, and the carpeting *Thymus serpyllum* and its varieties in shades of mauve, pink and white flowers, which are most loved by bees, and the Corsican mint, *Mentha requienii*, are strongly aromatic prostrate plants. This mint forms a thin veil of light green with tiny mauve flowers.

For a cool corner *Hutchinsia alpina* will form a green mat covered from May onwards with little white flowers, and for quite a different position that is dry and in full sun, there are various houseleeks, or sempervivums. The floriferous alpine phloxes and *Saxifraga aizoon* and its forms are also useful, and *Potentilla tonguei*, which bears rich apricot, crimson-blotched flowers on 5-in (13-cm) stems off and on throughout the summer.

Where there is a wide paved terrace or patio it may be possible to introduce one or two dwarf conifers, such as the erect, always admired Noah's Ark juniper, *Juniperus communis compressa*, but care should be taken not to overdo the planting of these dwarfs. Some are of prostrate habit but are vigorous and will eventually cover quite a considerable area so they must be planted only where there is ample space. If a specimen is placed a few feet back from a broad path or terrace it will make an attractive evergreen carpet and will not then encroach too much over the actual paving.

Sited at the end of a formal terrace or wide-paved path the golden Irish yew (*Taxus baccata fastigiata aurea*) will make a striking erect column with an eventual height of about 15 ft (4.5 m). The golden sheen is pleasing throughout the year. If something less formal is desired, perhaps to associate with a nearby bed of hardy heathers, then the dwarf form of the European mountain pine, *Pinus mugo pumilio*, makes a dense spreading rather Japanese-looking little tree about 2 ft (60 cm) in height. It is very hardy and does not object to lime in the soil.

The ingenious gardener will find many ways of making a path or terrace colourful and interesting, rather than just a stretch of stone to provide a footway from A to B.

Chrysanthemums for Display

With the exception of the rose, few plants have been developed more extensively or over so long a period as the chrysanthemum. As a result it is a wonderfully varied flower with all kinds of forms and colours, and a flowering season which, even without the aid of artificially controlled day length, extends from July to January. The later varieties require the protection of a greenhouse to preserve their flowers from injury by frost, but this still leaves a period of three or four months during which chrysanthemums can play a very important part in the open garden.

For this purpose they possess a quality that is often overlooked, the ability to withstand, far better than most plants, the shock of being transplanted when fully grown. The Pompon and Korean varieties are particularly good in this respect. This means that it is possible to keep chrysanthemums in reserve until they are really needed; to grow them, perhaps, in the vegetable garden or in some other place where they will not need to be decorative, and then to remove them to the display beds just as they are about to come into bloom. This can be a very useful method of filling up gaps caused by the removal of earlier flowering plants.

There is a bewilderingly large number of varieties but a great many of these are not suitable for garden display. They either flower too late, or they have flowers that are readily damaged by rain, or they have been specially bred to produce large flowers for show or for cutting. For the garden it is quantity rather than size of bloom that really matters. The Pompon varieties with their tight little flowers can be far more effective than some of the show varieties that will produce only five or six big blooms to each plant. Single-flowered and double-flowered chrysanthemums of the so-called Korean type are excellent display plants and they will go on flowering outdoors a good deal later than most. All the same some of the larger flowered varieties can be used if they have good firm petals, and there can be no denying that what they lack in mass display they fully make up for in the individual beauty of their flowers.

Propagation

For whatever purpose chrysanthemums are being grown the method of starting them off is the same. Young shoots are removed from old plants, are prepared as cuttings and are then rooted in a greenhouse or frame. If no such facilities are available it is possible to grow chrysanthemums from what are sometimes called Irishman's cuttings, i.e. shoots pulled from old plants with a few roots attached. This method works quite well with many of the free growing Korean and Rubellum varieties, but is not so satisfactory for the more highly developed varieties with large flowers. Ordinary cuttings are taken in February and March. Irishman's cuttings need not be taken until April and can go straight into a bed of well-broken soil in the open. The true cuttings must be prepared as I have already described for other cuttings, and are best rooted in a propagating frame or a box covered with a sheet of glass and placed in the greenhouse. As soon as they are rooted and start to grow, they must either be planted 2 or 3 in (5 to 8 cm) apart in shallow boxes, or be potted individually in 3- or 3½-in (8- or 9-cm) pots. In either case John Innes potting compost No. 1 or a soilless compost can be used.

Soon after this the chrysanthemums must be put in an unheated frame where they will remain for two or three weeks to be hardened off before being planted out. This may be in late April or early May.

Planting in the Garden

At this stage there are two possibilities, either to plant where the chrysanthemums are to flower, or to plant in a reserve bed from which they will be removed to the flowering positions when they are required there. In either case the ground must be well dug and fed with a good general fertilizer scattered over the surface at about 4 oz per square yard (110 g per square metre).

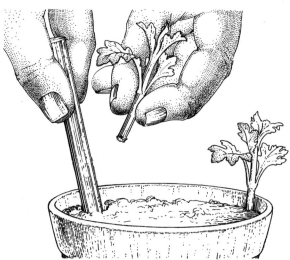

Rooting chrysanthemum cuttings: Use sturdy shoots about 3 in (8 cm) long, remove lower leaves and trim stem below a joint. Then dip base of cuttings in hormone rooting powder. Insert cuttings around the edge of a 3-in (8-cm) pot and afterwards place in a propagating frame or a box covered with a sheet of glass

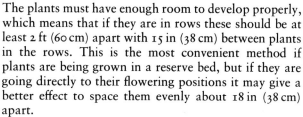

The plants must have enough room to develop properly, which means that if they are in rows these should be at least 2 ft (60 cm) apart with 15 in (38 cm) between plants in the rows. This is the most convenient method if plants are being grown in a reserve bed, but if they are going directly to their flowering positions it may give a better effect to space them evenly about 18 in (38 cm) apart.

Stake them immediately so that their stems can be properly tied in from the outset. Chrysanthemum growth is brittle and easily broken by wind. One cane or strong stick to each plant will suffice, and it need be no taller than the advertised height of the plants – about 2 ft (60 cm) for most Korean, Rubellum and Pompon varieties, and 3 ft (1 m) for the larger flowered varieties. Then when the supports have been pushed well into the soil and the stems have grown up around them they will be concealed from view.

After planting out, the tip of each plant should be pinched out to make it produce side growths. Subsequently the tips of these can also be removed to make the plants even more bushy.

Aftercare

During the following months the plants must be sprayed occasionally to keep them clear of greenfly (aphid), capsid bugs and other pests, the soil around them must be hoed to kill weeds, and an occasional feed should be given. Malathion and dimethoate will take care of the pests and any good general fertilizer can be used as a feed.

Books on chrysanthemum cultivation usually have a lot to say about disbudding and timing. Neither need trouble the gardener who is simply growing for display, unless some large flowers are wanted, in which case some disbudding will be needed. This means that the natural tendency of the chrysanthemum to produce its flowers in sprays, not all opening at the same time, must be controlled by removing all the side buds or shoots and only leaving one central flower bud on each stem to develop. The time to do this is as soon as the flower buds can be seen, at which stage they will be tight and green and not much bigger than a large pin's head. The surrounding buds, or any shoots appearing lower down the stems, are then rubbed or pinched out or removed with the point of a knife. It is rather a fiddling job which the enthusiastic chrysanthemum grower thoroughly enjoys, for in each tiny bud he can foresee the splendid bloom that is going to materialize. But as I have already said, if you are growing chrysanthemums simply for mass display, it is best to forget all about disbudding.

If the chrysanthemums are grown in a reserve bed a sharp spade should be thrust into the soil in a circle about 9 in (23 cm) from the base of the plant to sever far-reaching roots. Do this a week before lifting and then, a day before lifting, water the plants thoroughly. Lift and replant with as little delay as possible. It is as well to prepare the holes for the plants before starting to lift them. Round off the whole operation by treading the soil firmly around the roots, raking the surface level and giving a good watering in.

'Stool' Plants to Provide Cuttings

When the plants have finished flowering most of them can be discarded, but a few of each variety should be carefully labelled with name and colour, lifted and boxed or planted in a frame to provide cuttings for next year. As each 'stool' plant is capable of giving 10 to 20 good cuttings it will be seen that not many are required.

Opposite. Top: Fairie, a dwarf pompon chrysanthemum. Bottom left: Bill Else, an early-flowering intermediate chrysanthemum. Bottom right: Goya, an early-flowering reflexed decorative chrysanthemum

Dahlias for Display

The dahlia is a magnificent display plant, for it flowers consistently, continuously and freely from mid-summer until the first real frosts of the autumn, and is available in a vast array of colours, shapes and sizes. There are brilliant colours, rich colours, delicate colours, in fact something to suit every need and taste. You can have tall dahlias for the back of a border or short dahlias for the front, with every intermediate height for use where it is required. There are spiky flowers and round flowers, shaggy flowers and smooth flowers, each type available in a whole assortment of sizes.

I like the small and medium-sized dahlias and have no room for the giant-flowered varieties – at any rate in the display garden. It is a pity that so many people, having seen these monsters at shows, seem to think of them as typical of all dahlias.

Classification

Because of this great diversity in dahlias and the vast numbers of varieties that have been raised, it has been necessary to devise groupings and classifications for them. A few of the names chosen for these groups could be a little misleading to the uninitiated. All the spiky-flowered kinds are called Cactus or Semi-cactus dahlias though they do not look remotely like any cactus. A lot of the flatter petalled types are called Decoratives, and so they are, but it should not be supposed that other types are not equally decorative in the garden. The dwarf dahlias, up to about 2 ft (60 cm) in height, are called Bedding dahlias, but again it should not be assumed from this that they are the only ones suitable for filling beds. It just depends what you want in the bed, a short plant or a tall one.

Dahlias with globular flowers less than 2 in (5 cm) in diameter are called Pompons; above this size they are called Ball dahlias, and can be up to 6 in (15 cm) across.

You will find all these types amply described in the catalogues of nurserymen who deal in dahlias, with plenty of varieties of each from which to choose, and as nearly all dahlias today are good (they have to be or they soon get superseded by more worthy ones) you can really take your pick according to your fancy.

Troubles

The dahlia is a very easy plant to grow as it thrives in most soils and is not greatly troubled by pests and diseases. Aphids and capsid bugs can attack leaves and flower buds, but are easily destroyed by occasional spraying with menazon, malathion, or dimethoate. Earwigs may disfigure some of the flowers, but are really more of a problem to would-be exhibitors than to display gardeners to whom an occasional faulty petal is not a major disaster. BHC or derris powder will deal with them and with caterpillars.

The only real weakness of the dahlia is its addiction to virus diseases which weaken rather than destroy it. Most varieties contract virus of some kind after a time, but some are relatively unaffected by it. Others gradually decline and are replaced by new varieties, which partly accounts for the ever-changing names in the dahlia lists. There is not a cure for dahlia virus, so if you find a plant in your beds that is stunted, or has foliage mottled with yellow, it is best to have it out at once and burn it before the trouble is spread by aphids and capsid bugs to other plants.

Propagation

Dahlias, like chrysanthemums, can be grown from cuttings taken in spring. If old plants are placed close

Dahlias provide one of the boldest and brightest flower displays of the summer. They are available in a multitude of flower shapes and colours and are represented here by the small cactus dahlia Salmon Rays

together in boxes in February or March, covered with any light soil or peat, placed in the greenhouse in a temperature of 13°C to 18°C (55°F to 65°F) and kept moist they will soon start to make a lot of new shoots. These can be severed, close to the parent plant, when 3 to 4 in (8 to 10 cm) long and trimmed, prepared and inserted just like chrysanthemum cuttings (see p. 105). When rooted they are potted singly, again just like chrysanthemums, and soon after this are removed to a frame in which they can be given more and more ventilation until they are hardy enough, and the weather is mild enough, for them to go outdoors.

As dahlias are much more tender than chrysanthemums, this planting out will be correspondingly later; towards the end of May in the milder areas of Britain, but early in June over most of the rest of the country.

Planting in the Garden

Unlike chrysanthemums, dahlias do not take kindly to being moved when they are fully grown, so they must go straight into their flowering positions. They like the soil to be rich and reasonably open. Manure or garden compost can be dug in freely before they are planted, and the surface can also be dusted with a good general fertilizer. Then the plants are carefully tapped out of their pots and planted, without root disturbance. The short varieties can be spaced 18 in (45 cm) apart, the medium to tall ones 2 to 3 ft (60 cm to 1 m).

This is the way with dahlias grown from cuttings, but there is an alternative method which will suit those gardeners who have no glass. The dahlia has tuberous roots which can be stored in a dry, frostproof place all the winter. These roots can be planted out of doors in late April or early May. Covered with 2 or 3 in (5 or 8 cm) of soil they will be quite safe from the occasional night frosts we are likely to get during May, and by the

time their shoots are through the soil the danger of frost should be over. As tubers produce more shoots than cuttings do, they should be given more space, at least 2 ft (60 cm) for the dwarfs, 4 to 5 ft (1·25 to 1·5 m) for the tall ones.

Dahlias make heavier growth than chrysanthemums and it is even more brittle, so stakes must be strong and ties fairly frequent. One-inch-square wood stakes are sold for the purpose, and if treated with copper naphthanate will last for years.

Spraying, hoeing and feeding are the same as for chrysanthemums (see previous chapter). The small- and medium-flowered varieties need not be disbudded for good display, but it is necessary to look over the plants frequently to remove faded flowers which look untidy and, if they produce seed, shorten the flowering season.

Storing the Tubers

That is all that needs to be done until a frost arrives in autumn, sharp enough to blacken the dahlia flowers and leaves. This is the signal that the season is at an end and that it is time to cut all stems back to within about 9 in (23 cm) of soil level; tie a label to each plant, dig up the roots carefully and dry them off for a few days in some frostproof place. The ideal is to place them upside down on the greenhouse staging, but if this is not possible they can go into a shed or a spare room. Then, when they are thoroughly dry, all remaining soil is knocked off them and the roots are packed into boxes and stored away in any place that is dry and cool but frostproof. A cupboard is often as good a place as any, but do not pack your dahlia tubers too near the hot water cylinder or they may shrivel up before it is time to start them into growth again the following year. In any case it is wise to inspect the tubers occasionally for signs of rotting; dusting with flowers of sulphur will help to prevent moulds developing.

Dahlias make very heavy and brittle growth so when planting them out in the garden it is important to make sure that they are adequately staked

Taking a dahlia cutting: Tubers are started into growth in February or March, the young shoots being removed when 3 to 4 in (8 to 10 cm) long and treated as cuttings

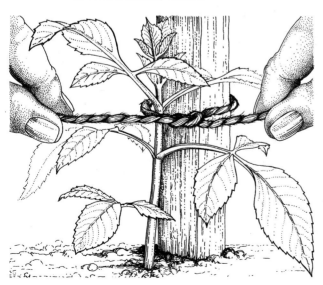

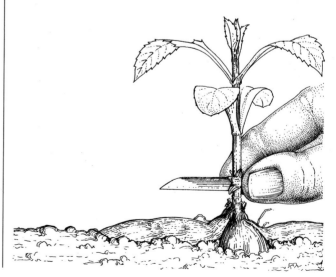

Brightening Shady Corners

There are quite a number of plants that enjoy shade, so the problem of coping with such conditions is not really as difficult as many gardeners seem to imagine. I am not thinking now of a plot of poorly drained soil at the base of a high north-facing wall where no sun ever penetrates, but of a bed, say, of reasonably fertile soil that gets some sun at some period of the day. If the soil has been neglected, the first thing to do is to attempt to improve its fertility. Fork it over a week or two before planting, removing any perennial weeds, and work in some hop manure or peat which will help to retain moisture and give the plants something into which to root. Bonemeal applied at the rate of about 2 oz to the square yard (55 g to the square metre) is a useful slow-acting fertilizer. Should the soil be wet and sticky fork in sharp sand, brick dust or even old sifted ashes, which will help to break up the soil and improve the drainage. If ashes are used they must have weathered in the open for not less than three or four months, so do not use ashes straight from the grate. Should there be any well-rotted garden compost available this will provide valuable plant food, and it should be forked in a few inches below the surface or be used as a mulch.

Hardy Perennial Plants for Shade

Aconitum (Monkshood). Several species and varieties of aconitum thrive in moist soil and shade. The 3-ft (1-m) spikes of blue flowers in summer are delightful. The blue and white Blue Sceptre, the deep blue Newry Blue and the violet-blue Bressingham Spire are good modern hybrids.

Anemone. The Japanese anemones (varieties of *A. hybrida*, often listed erroneously as *A. japonica*), include shades of pink, rose, ruby, and white. There are double and semi-double varieties of these late summer-flowering plants which vary from 2 to 4 ft (60 cm to 1·25 m) high. See p. 40 for suggested varieties.

Aquilegia (Columbine). Long-spurred hybrid aquilegias are old favourites in shades of pink, crimson, purple and blue, flowering in May and June on 2½-ft (75-cm) stems. They may also be grown in full sun so long as the soil does not dry out, but the flowering season is not there so long. The 2-ft (60-cm) tall Crimson Star is a charming crimson and white, free-flowering hybrid.

Astilbe. These spiraea-like plants with dainty foliage and graceful plumes of red, pink or white flowers are a joy in summer, and are more fully described on pp. 40 and 115.

Bergenia. Useful edging plants with thick leathery leaves and short spikes of pink, red and white flowers in March and April. Height 1 ft (30 cm). See also p. 40.

Bleeding Heart, see Dicentra

Bronze Leaf, see Rodgersia

Brunnera. Perhaps better known as *Anchusa myosotidiflora*, the blue forget-me-not-like flowers of *B. macrophylla* are borne in dainty sprays in June. Height 1 to 1½ ft (30 to 45 cm).

Christmas Rose, see Helleborus

Cimicifuga. In July and August the sprays of creamy-white flowers of *C. racemosa* are borne on 3½-ft (1·15-m) stems. The dainty foliage is also attractive.

Columbine, see Aquilegia

Convallaria (Lily-of-the-Valley). A fragrant, spring-flowering plant, preferring a moist position, which should be left undisturbed for several years after planting.

Day Lily, see Hemerocallis

Dead Nettle, see Lamium

Dicentra (Bleeding Heart, or Dutchman's Breeches). The handsome *D. spectabilis* bears sprays of pink and white flowers in May and June. It likes a sheltered corner where the soil is light and rich. The light green fern-like foliage is most attractive.

Digitalis (Foxglove). These seed themselves readily and will soon form a colony. The common foxglove is a biennial, as are the Excelsior Hybrids which have flowers all round the stem, and there are pure white foxgloves which show up well against a dark background.

Doronicum. The bright yellow *Doronicum* Harpur Crewe has been grown in gardens for many years and is full of flower during April and May. The deep yellow, double-flowered Spring Beauty flowers early on 18-in (45-cm) stems, which are shorter than those of some of the other varieties.

Dutchman's Breeches, see Dicentra

Epimedium. An attractive genus of plants with handsome foliage which turns a pleasing bronze and remains on the plant throughout the winter. *E. versicolor sulphureum* is the one most often grown and it bears its pale sulphur-yellow flowers in spring on 9-in (23-cm) stems. It is useful for suppressing weeds.

Foam Flower, see Tiarella

Foxglove, see Digitalis

Gentiana. The Willow Gentian, *G. asclepiadea*, has arching, 18-in (45-cm) stems, bearing dark blue flowers

in July and August. It likes a moist, leafy soil. There is also a white form.

Helleborus. The Christmas Rose, *H. niger*, and the Lenten Rose, *H. orientalis*, as well as *H. corsicus* and *H. foetidus*, thrive in shade and in a moist but well-drained soil. The long-lasting flowers, particularly of the Christmas rose, should be protected with a cloche in stormy weather.

Hemerocallis (Day Lily). Day lilies do best in a fairly moist soil, and they are described on p. 115.

Hosta (Plantain Lily). These are one of the best plants for fairly moist shade. They are described on pp. 46 and 115.

Kirengeshoma. The Japanese *K. palmata* bears charming tubular, drooping yellow flowers in the autumn on stems about 3 ft (1 m) high. The large, lobed leaves are also attractive for much of the year. It likes a moist, leafy soil.

Lamium. The creeping dead nettle, *L. maculatum*, is an attractive creeper with its green leaves striped with white down the centre. It is no more than 6 in (15 cm) high and has hooded pink flowers all summer. Particularly attractive is the golden-leaved variety *aureum*. It will grow in all soils but prefers those which are moist.

Lenten Rose, see Helleborus

Lily-of-the-Valley, see Convallaria

Mertensia. The Virginian cowslip, *M. virginica*, bears pendulous, blue, bell-shaped flowers on arching stems in May. The glaucous leaves are also attractive while they last. It grows up to 2 ft (60 cm) tall and requires plenty of moisture during the growing season.

Below left: *Dicentra spectabilis*
Below right: *Helleborus corsicus*

Opposite: The flower spikes of the foxglove (digitalis) are seen to perfection in the shade of a tree

Astilbes with their feathery plumes in shades of pink, cream and red are tolerant of shade and prefer shelter from strong sunshine which can dry out the soil. They are happiest at the edge of a pool or stream where their roots have access to ample supplies of moisture

Monkshood, see Aconitum

Omphalodes (Navel Wort). The sprays of deep blue forget-me-not-like flowers of *O. cappadocica* are borne on stems up to 9 in (23 m) high in May and June. It does best in a moist, well-drained soil and in light shade.

Periwinkle, see Vinca

Plantain Lily, see Hosta

Primula. For moist shady soils, few plants are more effective than the many sorts of primula. See p. 117.

Polygonatum (Solomon's Seal). With its clusters of pendulous white bells the Solomon's seal makes a graceful plant. These flowers are borne on arching stems up to 2½ ft (75 cm) long in June.

Rodgersia (Bronze Leaf). These handsome plants take some little time to become established but are well worth growing. The leaves of *R. aesculifolia* are similar to those of the horse chestnut, and plumes of fragrant, pinkish flowers appear in July. Height 3 ft (1 m).

Solomon's Seal, see Polygonatum

Tiarella (Foam Flower). The common name aptly describes *T. cordifolia*, for it bears little spikes of creamy-white flowers, pink in the bud stage, on 9-in (23-cm) stems from May to July. The heart-shaped leaves are also attractive and colourful in the autumn.

Trillium (Wood Lily). For moist woodland, trilliums are excellent, and are described on p. 117.

Vinca. Periwinkles are excellent plants for shady places, casting out their long stems to cover the ground with a thick mat. *V. major* is a dark-leaved evergreen and has blue flowers in both its ordinary and variegated forms. *V. minor* has smaller leaves and a greater range of flower colours; these vary from white to blue and deep purple. Periwinkles will survive in most soils and can be clipped back if they become too invasive.

Virginian Cowslip, see Mertensia

Wood Lily, see Trillium

Waterside Plants for Colour

Many waterside or bog plants are most colourful, and if thought is given to their siting, remarkable beautiful effects may be achieved by reflections in the water, particularly that of a placid pool. But the colour should not be overdone, or it will destroy the cool restfulness one associates with water in the garden. The feathery heads of pink, crimson or white astilbes standing above the mass of handsome green foliage will be doubly effective when seen across a pool, and the elegant heads of the Japanese *Iris kaempferi* are serenely beautiful when growing beside water. Generally speaking, planting is best done in early spring and the finest effect is produced with bold clumps of one variety, rather than dotting odd specimens here and there. The number in each group will, of course, depend upon the size of the pool or the length of the stream.

Hardy Waterside Plants

Astilbe. These graceful plants are often confused with spiraeas. They thrive in moist soil beside and above water-level in sun or partial shade. There are a number of popular named varieties with flower spikes about 2½ to 3 ft (75 cm to 1 m) in height, and the main period of flowering is in July and August. An imposing tall Chinese species is *A. davidii*, with long spikes of rose-lavender flowers in July and August from 4 to 6 ft (1·25 to 2 m) high. There are also dwarf species for a cool, moist corner on the rock garden, such as *A. glaberrima saxosa* with rosy-pink plumes which it bears on 4-in (10-cm) stems in late summer.

Caltha (Marsh Marigold or Kingcup). One of the earliest plants to flower in the water garden, *C. palustris* bears rich golden flowers on 12-in (30-cm) stems and the leaves are dark green and glossy. There are various forms including a fine double variety with long-lasting flowers, *C. p. plena*.

Day Lily, see Hemerocallis

Giant Cow Parsnip, see Heracleum

Globe Flower, see Trollius

Gunnera. Where there is sufficient space the handsome leaves of *G. manicata* are a spectacular sight. A rich soil is required and the crowns must be protected in autumn and throughout the winter with a covering of bracken or straw.

Hemerocallis (Day Lily). Day lilies have been much improved in recent years and there are now some hybrids with very attractive colouring to plant in a moist, wild garden. The colour range is from pale yellow to mahogany-crimson. They associate well with astilbes, hostas and the like. Flowering over a long period from June to September, they are in their full glory in July and August. Most are 2½ to 3 ft (75 cm to 1 m) tall.

Heracleum. Given sufficient space, the giant cow parsnip, *H. mantegazzianum*, with its large leaves and large flat heads of white flowers in summer is a plant to provide interest in the middle distance of streamside plantings. But it is 10 ft (3 m) tall and nearly as much across so only suitable for spacious settings. Also, if well suited, it can seed itself freely – so use with discretion.

Hosta (Plantain Lily). These are admirable for planting near water where their large, prominently veined, cool-looking leaves are most effective. There are many different species and varieties, some with glaucous, others with variegated, foliage. They include *H. undulata* with green and white leaves and *H. fortunei* with glaucous-green leaves. Once planted they should be left undisturbed to form large clumps. The funnel-shaped flowers are borne on stems from 1 to 3 ft (30 cm to 1 m) in height and are in shades of lilac, mauve, pale purple and white. They like partial shade although they will flourish in sun so long as the soil, which should be rich, does not dry out. See also p. 46.

Iris. A very large genus, some of which are waterside plants. Among the better known are the Japanese *I. kaempferi* with elegant flat heads of velvety flowers in shades of violet, purple, plum, yellow and white, borne in July on erect stems 2 ft (60 cm) or more in height. They require a lime-free soil, as does the rich blue *I. laevigata* which will grow in water about 3 in (8 cm) deep, or on the water's edge where its roots can go down below water level. The dainty *I. sibirica* is a delight in June with its bluish-purple flowers on slender 3-ft (1-m) stems. There are several good named hybrids, the flowers of Perry's Blue being a most attractive sky-blue colour with a touch of white on the falls, while Caesar is a large, violet-purple. Where space permits the yellow

Water adds another dimension to the garden and extends the range of plants that can be grown. Water-lilies and other aquatics find a home in the water and bog plants delight in the moist soil at the waterside

flag, *Iris pseudacorus*, is worth planting in shallow water or on the brink of water. This is the iris that may be seen growing wild in ponds and ditches. The flowers open one at a time and continue throughout May and June on stems up to about 3 ft (1 m) high.

Kingcup, see Caltha

Lysichitum (Skunk Cabbage). The yellow-flowered *L. americanum* has most striking arum-like flowers which it bears in April and these are followed by enormous deep green leaves. The flowers have a foul smell and should never be cut for use indoors. It is perfectly hardy and revels in thick mud at the water's edge. There is also a white species, *L. camtschatcense*, which flowers a few weeks later. Both are plants for a large garden.

Marsh Marigold, see Caltha

Mimulus (Musk). These gay moisture-loving plants produce a profusion of flower throughout the summer. There are numerous species and varieties, both perennial

Iris laevigata **and its forms will actually grow in water**

Hostas are excellent waterside plants

and annual, the latter being easily raised from seed sown in damp soil at the water's edge. The markings on the little trumpet-like flowers in shades of orange, yellow, red and pink are delightful, and there are self-coloured varieties.

Osmunda. The Royal Fern, *Osmunda regalis*, is a magnificent spectacle with its large, handsome fronds, perhaps 4 ft (1·25 m) in length, swaying beside a pool. When planted on a small mound surrounded by boggy soil it thrives luxuriantly. Planting is best done in the spring just when growth starts. It will grow in partial shade or in sun so long as the roots have adequate moisture.

Plantain Lily, see Hosta

Primula. A very large genus, many of which thrive in bog gardens. Once established some of the varieties will seed themselves happily and soon form colourful colonies. They like moisture at the roots but should not be 'stuck in the mud'. One of the earliest to flower, in April, is *Primula rosea*, with bright pink flowers on 6-in (15-cm) stems above tufts of pale green leaves. This is a real bog plant. Earlier still is *P. denticulata*. This species, with its globular, mauve flowers, and its white form, *alba,* do not require so much moisture to sustain their 12-in (30-cm) stems. The flowers of this primula appear from March to May. Growing taller, up to 18 in (45 cm), *P. beesiana*, with fragrant rosy-carmine flower heads, and *P. bulleyana*, pale orange, are a delight from May onwards. These and *P. florindae* often seed themselves

with abandon. The soft yellow, drooping flowers of *P. florindae* are carried on 3-ft (1-m) stems in July and August. It will grow in sun or partial shade given plenty of moisture. Other bright species are *P. japonica* with tiers of pink, crimson or white flowers on 2-ft (60-cm) stems, and *P. pulverulenta*, which is similar but taller, and the whorls of flower are crimson. There are many beautiful hybrids known as the Bartley Strain in shades of pink, salmon, apricot and buff.

Royal Fern, see Osmunda

Skunk Cabbage, see Lysichitum

Trillium (Wood Lily). These spring-flowering woodland plants do well in partial shade and moist soil near, but above, the water. They like a rich leafy soil and once planted should be left undisturbed. *T. grandiflorum*, the Wake Robin, has large pure white three-petalled flowers and there are other North American species, some of which are still rare in cultivation.

Trollius (Globe Flower). *T. europaeus* has large globe-shaped pale yellow flowers on 18-in (45-cm) stems from May onwards and there are some splendid hybrids, see p. 51. Given plenty of moisture at the roots they will present no difficulty in cultivation.

Wake Robin, see Trillium

Wood Lily, see Trillium

Studies in Grey

Silver-foliaged herbaceous and shrubby plants, carefully sited in a garden, paying special attention to their background, can be most effective over a long period. Generally speaking these plants like a sunny position and a well-drained soil, and growing in the sun they stand out in all their beauty against a background of evergreens or, failing this, tall herbaceous plants with large green leaves. They will also show up well in the sun against a dark-wooded fence.

Where something fairly bold is required, *Senecio laxifolius* will make a handsome shrub of about 3 ft (1 m) in height, broadly spreading in habit and perhaps 6 ft (2 m) wide. It is evergrey, and in the summer has many sprays of yellow daisy-like flowers. Sprigs of this plant are most effective when used in floral decorations, particularly with dianthus or pinks which associate so happily with grey-foliaged plants.

The lavender cotton, *Santolina incana*, also has yellow flowers, in this case little buttons, and the silvery-grey foliage is aromatic. It makes a neat little bush about 18 in (45 cm) high. There is a more compact form, known as *nana*, which hardly reaches 12 in (30 cm). The velvety texture of lamb's ear, or *Stachys lanata*, is delightful and it makes an excellent edging plant. Prostrate in habit, it suppresses weeds. The spikes of crimson flowers are almost covered in grey wool and are at their best in July and August. It presents no problems so far as soil is concerned, but prefers a dryish position. It is easily increased by division or by seed.

The silvery *Anaphalis triplinervis* thrives in sun or dry shade and makes a compact plant with densely woolly, silver-grey leaves and bunches of off-white little flowers on 15-in (38-cm) stems. The stems may be cut and will last well when dried.

There are several attractive artemisias, some with aromatic foliage. It is the foliage rather than the flowers that is effective. With stems up to about 4 ft (1.25 m) high, *Artemisia ludoviciana*, with its woolly white foliage, is a useful plant towards the back of the border or for cutting and using in large arrangements. About half that height is *A. nutans* with feathery silver spikes, and Silver Queen is another pleasing variety with stems about 2½ ft (75 cm) high.

Where the soil is poor and dry, plant the artemisia which is commonly called dusty miller, *A. stelleriana,* which has finely cut silvery foliage and small yellow flowers on stems about 1 ft (30 cm) in height. It has become naturalized on sandy soil in parts of south-west England.

The spiky foliage or 'grass' of the dianthus family is pleasing even in the winter months, and such old friends as Mrs Sinkins, among many others, will clothe the ground with silvery-grey. Then in June and July there is the spicy fragrance of the charming blooms. The smaller alpine pinks are delightful for the rock garden, and *Alyssum saxatile* makes a bold display with its heads of bright yellow flowers and its grey leaves in early May. The variety *citrinum* has fluffy heads of pale lemon-yellow.

Also for a sunny, really dry place on a rock garden the trailing *Antirrhinum asarina* is effective, with grey leaves and ivory-yellow flowers with a yellow throat. A native of Southern France, it does not like winter wet, but is worth taking a little trouble to cultivate.

Then there is lavender, catmint (*Nepeta faassenii*) and *Gypsophila paniculata*, or baby's breath, which makes a great mound of grey in the summer covered with a host of tiny white flowers. When cut it is charming with a vase of sweet peas, and if used with gladioli it covers the rigid stems and makes the whole effect lighter.

In late summer the silvery-grey *Perovskia atriplicifolia*, with its slender spikes of soft blue flowers, is most decorative. The stems are erect and about 4 ft (1.25 m) high. This shrub is commonly called Russian sage and likes a sunny place and a well-drained soil. Planted on top of a retaining wall it is quite outstanding. Also belonging to the sage family is the shrub *Phlomis fruticosa*, or Jerusalem sage, which has woolly leaves and rusty-

Above: The effectiveness of the silvered foliage of *Senecio laxifolius* is increased by the charming heads of yellow daisies which appear from June to August

Below: *Stachys lanata* Silver Carpet sets off perfectly the succulent pale green foliage and dusky pink flowers of *Sedum spectabile*

yellow flowers. These last are borne in summer on 3-ft (1-m) stems.

Among the most glorious grey-foliaged plants are the romneyas. They are not easy to get established but once they have rooted into a light, warm, well-drained soil which is to their liking, they show their approval by a magnificent display of large flowers from July to September every year. One of the two species is *Romneya coulteri*, the California tree poppy, which is the one that is more often grown, with blue-grey leaves and satiny white flowers about 4 in (10 cm) across with a conspicuous mass of golden stamens. Very similar, *R. trichocalyx* is less branching and not so tall. Once planted, romneyas should be left undisturbed and they will spread by means of underground roots.

There is a strange little Australian shrub known as *Calocephalus brownii*, or cushion bush, which is suitable for growing in a frost-free greenhouse. It forms a rigid plant about 1 ft (30 cm) high, densely covered with silvery-grey foliage. It is useful in summer for window boxes or for planting out in front of a border, but must be lifted and given protection during the winter or it will not survive.

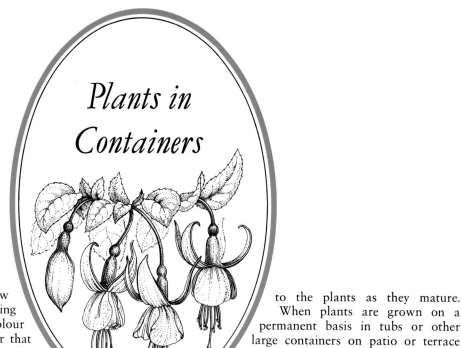

Plants in Containers

Plant containers such as window boxes, balcony boxes, tubs, hanging baskets and the like will bring colour where space is restricted, or for that matter to a terrace, patio or roof garden. So far as window boxes are concerned the size is naturally controlled by the dimensions of the sill upon which it is to stand. It should not be less than 6 in (15 cm) deep and as broad as is feasible, for the smaller the box the quicker it will dry out during hot weather, and that means more watering. All sorts of boxes are available, hardwood, rustic elm, and teak as well as lightweight polystyrene troughs, in different sizes and in a wide range of prices.

Any such container must have drainage holes in the bottom, for otherwise the soil will become sour. Most boxes and tubs made for this purpose have such holes, but it is as well to make sure. The holes must be covered with broken pieces of flower pot, commonly called 'crocks', placed hollow side downwards over the holes to prevent them from becoming clogged with soil. Over these should be spread a thin layer of small pebbles or moss litter to a depth of about 1 in (2·5 m). If the box is large and deep enough, old pieces of turf placed grass side downwards will provide more nourishment and moisture for the plant's roots.

The Soil Mixture

This brings me to the all-important question of soil which may not be an easy matter for flat dwellers, and those with town houses. It is a waste of time to fill boxes with poor, infertile soil dug from some corner of a town garden. The simplest way is to buy a bag of John Innes potting compost, sufficient for your needs, or where there are the facilities for preparing a compost use the following: 3 parts good loam, 2 parts well-rotted leafmould or granulated peat, and 1 part sharp sand (all parts by volume). A liberal handful of bonemeal should be added to each bushel of soil. This is a slow-acting fertilizer which will gradually become available to the plants as they mature.

When plants are grown on a permanent basis in tubs or other large containers on patio or terrace (see list of suggested plants on p. 122) then the top few inches of compost should be carefully removed each spring and replaced with a fresh mixture to provide the necessary sustenance. If you intend growing rhododendrons, azaleas, camellias or other lime-hating plants in this way remember, too, that the John Innes potting compost used must be without its usual lime content (such mixtures are freely available); or use some other soil mixture which takes account of this need. The container should be filled to within about an inch of the top, and the soil pressed firmly but gently to ensure that the corners and space along the sides are well filled. The soil should, of course, be moist but not wet.

Hanging Baskets

Stout wire hanging baskets are usually suspended by three chains or wires from a hook. Be sure that such a hook is firmly fixed, because a basket filled with soil and plants is surprisingly heavy. The basket is lined with fresh, damp moss which must be laid thickly enough to retain the soil within the basket. Use sturdy plants, preferably pot grown, and water them well an hour or so before putting them into the basket. Knock the plants out of the pots, and, if the plant is well-rooted, loosen the roots gently to assist them to grow quickly into the new compost. A medium-sized basket will take three plants that have been grown in 5-in (13-cm) pots, and probably three or more that have been grown in 3½-in (9-cm) pots. Where young plants of trailing lobelia are used, these can be placed hanging downwards by pushing the ball of roots up into the basket between the wires and then firmly pressing the moss and soil around the roots. Ivy-leaved geraniums are very suitable for planting in the top because as they grow they will trail over the sides.

Selecting Plants

When buying plants, particularly those grown in boxes, avoid those that are 'leggy' or starved and with yellowing leaves. Choose young, bushy plants with healthy green foliage – the others will give disappointing results and are not cheap at any price.

Spring-flowering Plants

Many of these can be bought in bud or in bloom in the early spring ready for planting out in window boxes and tubs.

Bellis perennis (Button daisy), pink, red and white. 6 in (15 cm), April.

Cheiranthus allionii (Siberian wallflower). Orange, 9 to 12 in (23 to 30 cm), April and May.

Myosotis (Forget-me-not). Royal Blue is an outstanding variety. 8 in (20 cm), May.

Pansies. Various beautiful colours. 6 in (15 cm), April, May onwards.

Polyanthuses. Many bright colours. 8 in (20 cm), April and May.

Primula E. R. Janes. Rose-pink. 3 in (8 cm), March.

Primula Wanda. Rich purple-crimson. 4 in (10 cm), March.

Stocks, East Lothian. Many beautiful colours. Fragrant. 12 to 18 in (30 to 45 cm), May.

Stocks, Brompton. A fine range of colours. 1 to 2 ft (30 to 60 cm), May.

Summer-flowering Plants

Many of these can be bought as small plants ready for planting out in containers in mid-May:

Ageratum Imperial Dwarf Blue. 9 in (23 cm), July to September.

Antirrhinum nanum. Various colours. 15 in (38 cm), July to September.

Begonias. Red, orange, pink and white. 8 to 12 in (20 to 30 cm), July to October.

Calceolarias (dwarf varieties). Yellow and brown. 12 in (30 cm), June to October.

Calendulas (Marigold). Yellow and orange. 12 to 18 in (30 to 45 cm), May to September.

Celosias (Cockscombs). Red and yellow. 18 in (45 cm), summer.

Centaurea (Cornflower). Blue and pink. 12 in (30 cm), June to August.

Chrysanthemums (annual varieties). Various colours. 1 to 3 ft (30 cm to 1 m), July to September.

Convolvulus major. Blue, pink and white. 12 in (30 cm), July to September.

Dahlias (Dwarf bedding). Various colours. 12 to 18 in (30 to 45 cm), July to October.

Fuchsias. Pink, rose and purple. 1 to 2 ft (30 to 60 cm), July to September.

Heliotropes (Cherry pie). Mauve and purple. 12 to 18 in (30 to 45 cm), June to September.

Hydrangeas, crimson, pink and blue. 1 to 3 ft (30 cm to 1 m), summer.

Lobelias. Blue and white. 12 in (30 cm), and trailing varieties, June to October.

Marguerites. White and yellow. 1 to 2 ft (30 to 60 cm), June to October.

Nasturtium. Golden, yellow, scarlet and maroon. 6 to 12 in (15 to 30 cm), and trailing, July to October.

Pansies. Various bright colours. 6 in (15 cm), May to September.

Pelargoniums (Geraniums). Many colours. 12 to 18 in (30 to 45 cm), June to September.

Penstemons. Various colours. 1 to 2 ft (30 to 60 cm), June to September.

Petunias. Various bright colours. 6 to 12 in (15 to 30 cm), June to September.

Phlox drummondii (dwarf). Crimson, pink, purple and white. 6 to 9 in (15 to 23 cm), July to October.

Stocks, Ten-week. Various colours. 15 to 18 in (38 to 45 cm), July to August.

Tagetes (African marigold). Bright yellow. 12 in (30 cm), July to October.

Ursinias. Bright orange. 9 to 12 in (23 to 30 cm), June to July.

Violas. Mauve, purple and white. 6 to 9 in (15 to 23 cm), May to July.

Summer flowers are almost brought into the house with this well-planted window box. Petunias, pelargoniums and marguerites are complemented by the yellow flowers and trailing foliage of *Lysimachia nummularia*

Bulbous Plants

Chionodoxas (Glory of the snow). Rich blue. March.
Crocuses. Purple, yellow and white. March.
Daffodils. Golden-yellow. March and April.
Hyacinths, in variety. April.
Iris reticulata. Rich violet. February and March.
Muscari (Grape hyacinth). Sky-blue. April.
Scillas (Dwarf squills). Deep blue. March.
Snowdrops, white. February.
Tulips (Double and Early Single varieties). April.

Permanent Plants for Containers

All the shrubs and climbers referred to below will give a fine display if well watered and fed weekly in the growing season.
Camellias. Shades of red, pink and white, March onwards.
Clematis. Large-flowered varieties in many colours from purple through blue, red and pink to white, from May onwards. Also *Clematis·montana* with white flowers in May, a tall growing and vigorous climber.
Choisya ternata. Fragrant white flowers in late spring and early summer, 4 to 6 ft (1·25 to 2 m).

Hanging baskets, wall-mounted pot holders, window boxes and troughs are used here to overcome the lack of a garden and are filled, almost entirely, with summer-flowering hardy and half-hardy annuals. Such containers can be replanted later with spring-flowering plants

Golden conifers. *Chamaecyparis lawsoniana aurea*, *Chamaecyparis pisifera aurea* and *Thuja occidentalis* Rheingold.
Hydrangeas. Crimson, pink and blue, 1 to 3 ft (30 cm to 1 m), summer.
Lonicera (Honeysuckle). May to June-flowering *Lonicera periclymenum belgica* (early Dutch honeysuckle) and *L. p. serotina* (late Dutch honeysuckle) flowering from July to October. The first has cream, red-flushed flowers, the second cream and reddish-purple.
Potentillas. Varieties of *Potentilla fruticosa*, shades of yellow, including coppery-yellow, and white, throughout summer and autumn.
Roses. Many varieties, including climbers (especially modern repeat-flowering varieties), hybrid teas and floribundas.
Rhododendrons and azaleas. Especially those rhododendrons classified as Hardy Hybrids (including crimson-scarlet Britannia, Purple Splendour and Pink Pearl), deciduous and evergreen azaleas. All demand lime-free soil.
Skimmia reevesiana (syn. *S. fortunei*). Long-persisting bright red fruits in autumn and winter, white flowers in May. 2½ ft (75 cm) tall.
Vinca major variegata. Pretty trailer for sun or shade with leaves marked with creamy-white; blue flowers in May.

Plants grown in small tubs and pots have the advantage of being portable and are ideal for use on the patio or terrace. Planted with standard fuchsias, tuberous begonias and other half-hardy plants, these can be moved around as frequently as required

Index

ACKNOWLEDGEMENTS

The publishers would like to thank the following for
the photographs used in this book:
Amateur Gardening, Pat Brindley, Ken Burras, John Cowley, Ernest Crowson,
Valerie Finnis, Leslie Johns, Sheila Orme, Robert Pearson, and
The Harry Smith Horticultural Photographic Collection.

Line drawings by Meg Rutherford